LIGHT OF LIFE

70 meditations for Easter

NICK FAWCETT

kevin mayhew

kevin
mayhew

First published in Great Britain in 2011 by Kevin Mayhew Ltd
Buxhall, Stowmarket, Suffolk IP14 3BW
Tel: +44 (0) 1449 737978 Fax: +44 (0) 1449 737834
E-mail: info@kevinmayhewltd.com

www.kevinmayhew.com

9 8 7 6 5 4 3 2 1 0

ISBN 978 1 84867 401 1

Catalogue No. 1501289

Cover design by Rob Mortonson
© Image used under licence from Shutterstock Inc.

Project managed by Free Range Book Design & Production

Printed and bound in Great Britain

Contents

About the author 7
Introduction 9

Easter

1 We had our spices ready to anoint his body – *Salome* 12
2 It was a bolt from the blue – *The other Mary* 14
3 The stone was rolled away – *Salome* 16
4 You'd have thought we'd be pleased, wouldn't you? – *Salome* 19
5 We thought he'd gone for ever – *Mary Magdalene* 22
6 They're not going to listen – *Mary Magdalene* 24
7 It seemed too good to be true – *Peter* 27
8 They said he was alive! – *Peter, James and John* 30
9 *Amazed? – Peter* 32
10 One look, that's all it took! – *The Apostle John* 34
11 I was shattered at the time – *Mary Magdalene* 37
12 I was distraught – *Mary Magdalene* 40
13 We met him, there on the Emmaus road – *Cleopas* 42
14 So that's who it was! – *Cleopas* 45
15 We were returning to Emmaus – *Cleopas* 48
16 It wasn't just the *doors* that were locked – *The Apostle James* 50
17 He was back! – *Peter* 52
18 We've seen Jesus! – *Andrew* 54
19 What's done cannot be undone, isn't that what they say? – *Bartholomew* 57
20 I wanted to know, that's all – *Thomas* 60
21 Did he condemn me for doubting? – *Thomas* 63
22 Would you believe it! – *Thomas* 65
23 I feel sorry for Thomas – *Matthew* 67
24 I thought I'd seen a ghost – *The Apostle James* 69
25 It was like the loaves and fishes all over again – *Nathanael* 72
26 We still hadn't seen it, you know – *Andrew* 74
27 How did we not see it before? – *Joanna, a companion of the disciples* 77
28 I'll never be able to say what it meant to me – *Mary Magdalene* 79
29 What were they playing at? – *Annas* 82
30 They don't know when they're beaten, do they? – *Caiaphas* 85

31 I just can't understand what happened
– *One of the guards at the tomb* 88
32 Three times he asked me – *Peter* 91
33 Why didn't he call someone like me? – *A shepherd* 94
34 To what lengths would I go in looking after my sheep?
– *A shepherd* 96
35 Why didn't he tell us who he was?
– *A Sadducee listening to Jesus* 98
36 We were confused when he first told us – *Thomas* 100
37 'Show us the Father,' I asked – *Philip* 102
38 He'd talked of his Father's house – *Philip* 104
39 He knew what was he was talking about, Jesus
– *A vineyard owner* 106
40 Oh no, not another rule to follow! – *Philip and Thomas* 108
41 There were things he felt unable to tell us at the time
– *Peter, James and John* 110
42 I couldn't help overhearing his words
– *The Apostle James* 113
43 What did he come to give us? – *The apostles* 115
44 We couldn't go where he was going – *Andrew* 117
45 He spoke with conviction, that man
– *Dionysius the Areopagite* 119
46 'What will it be like?' they ask me – *The Apostle Paul* 122
47 One day we'll see him again – *John the Evangelist* 125
48 I had a dream last night – *John the Evangelist* 128

Ascension Day

49 We had come, just as he'd told us to – *Matthew* 132
50 You'd think we'd have been dismayed, wouldn't you?
– *Philip* 135
51 Do you know what we did that day? – *Peter* 137
52 Surprised to see them there? – *Annas and Caiaphas* 139
53 We thought we'd lost him – *The Apostle James* 141
54 We stood there, speechless for a moment
– *The Apostle James* 143

Pentecost

55 We felt abandoned – *The Apostle John* 148
56 It happened, just as he had promised – *Peter* 150
57 A mighty wind, some point to – *The Apostle James* 152

58 'You will be my witnesses' – *The Apostle John* 154
59 Did it go to my head, becoming an apostle like that? – *Matthias* 157
60 We shouldn't have been surprised – *Peter* 159
61 I don't know who was the more surprised – *Peter* 161
62 It wasn't much of a gift – *Barnabas* 163
63 I have to tell you! – *Philip* 165
64 It was all so unnecessary – *The Apostle Paul* 168
65 He taught me the meaning of love – *The Apostle Paul* 171

Trinity Sunday

66 I didn't know if I was coming or going – *Nicodemus* 176
67 'What's in a name?' people ask – *Matthew* 178
68 I didn't know what he was on about at the time – *The Apostle John* 181
69 He's done the impossible – *The Apostle John* 184
70 He was just a man, that's what I thought – *Thomas* 187

Index of Key Themes 191
Index of Principal Characters 195
Index of Bible Passages 197

About the author

Nick Fawcett trained for the Baptist ministry at Bristol and Oxford, before going on to serve in pastorates in Leigh, Lancashire, and Gas Green, Cheltenham. He subsequently spent three years as a chaplain with the Christian movement Toc H, before deciding the time was right to commit himself to a writing ministry, supplementing his income through freelance editing. He has written over a hundred and twenty books, many of which have sold thousands of copies.

Together with their two children, Samuel and Kate, he lives with his wife, Deborah, in Wellington, Somerset, worshipping at the local Anglican church. A keen walker, gardener and chess player, as well as supporter of Southend United and local team Tiverton Town, Nick delights in the beauty of the Somerset and Devon countryside around his home, his numerous books owing much to the inspiration he unfailingly finds there.

Introduction

Those familiar with my writing will know what great store I set on using meditations to explore the meaning of Scripture. My interest in this medium began at a Good Friday service many years ago, built around reflective material written by various authors. Never having encountered such an approach before, I was spellbound, fascinated by the way familiar passages of Scripture and events from the life of Jesus suddenly spoke to me with new and unexpected power. This, I resolved, was a means of communication I needed to include in my own ministry. But when I looked for similar material covering other seasons of the Christian year or the wider message of the gospel, I struggled to find much that seemed suitable, to the point that I decided eventually the only solution was to write some myself. The opportunity came during a sabbatical, kindly allowed me by Gas Green Baptist Church during my time as minister there. In ten weeks I wrote a hundred meditations, subsequently published by Kevin Mayhew as my first book, *No Ordinary Man*, and since then I've produced a host of other books, many of which likewise use meditations to reflect on Scripture, life and faith.

In this book – one of a series for seasons of the Christian year – I've put together material from five books – *No Ordinary Man 1* and 2, and three volumes of *A Most Amazing Man* – to compile a comprehensive reflective resource for Easter, Ascension Day, Pentecost and Trinity Sunday. You'll find here numerous meditations – each carefully revised and arranged – linked to relevant passages of Scripture, including those recommended in the *Common Worship* lectionary for some of the later weeks of the Easter season.

How you use the book is, of course, entirely up to you. You may employ a single meditation alongside a sermon to reinforce its message, or perhaps even in place of the sermon altogether – say in a family service of some experimental act of worship. Alternatively, you may want to use several meditations to create a reflective service of your own aimed at presenting the message of one of these familiar seasons in a novel and arresting way. Or, of course, you may simply have bought this book as a tool for personal devotion. However you use it, my hope is that it will help to bring new meaning into the special seasons of this time of year; new insights into God's love so wonderfully revealed in Christ.

Nick Fawcett

With thanks to Alan Rutherford and Paul Tompsett
of Free Range Book Design & Production,
with whom its been such a pleasure to work on a host of books
over the past couple of years.

Easter

1

We had our spices ready to anoint his body

Salome

When the sabbath was over, Mary Magdalene, and Mary the mother of James, and Salome bought spices, so that they might go and anoint him. And very early on the first day of the week, when the sun had risen, they went to the tomb. They had been saying to one another, 'Who will roll away the stone for us from the entrance to the tomb?' When they looked up, they saw that the stone, which was very large, had already been rolled back.

Mark 16:1–4

Meditation

We had our spices ready to anoint his body,
a last gesture of devotion to our Lord,
but in all honesty we thought it would be a wasted journey,
for they'd rolled a mighty stone across the tomb
and set a guard to keep watch.
So why go, you ask?
Why waste our time on a fool's errand?
It's a fair question,
but what else were we to do?
We were numbed by grief, remember,
distraught and wretched beyond words.
And we needed to do something,
anything,
to dull the pain.
More than that, however stupid it may sound,
we wanted to be near Jesus,
dead though he was:
to feel that somehow the bond between us wasn't entirely broken.
If we could even approach the tomb,
view it from a distance,
it might help a little, we thought.

And who could say,
if the soldiers took pity on us,
perhaps they might even roll the stone away for a moment,
long enough for us to embalm his body as we had intended.
So we went,
hoping against hope,
yet not even in our wildest dreams daring to contemplate
what we found when we got there.
It was a wasted journey all right,
totally so, in one sense,
but not because we couldn't see his body.
Astonishingly,
incredibly,
there was no body to see!
The stone had been rolled away,
the tomb was empty –
Jesus was alive!

Prayer

Gracious God,
we praise you for the wonder of Easter,
we rejoice in the good news of Christ –
your victory, through him, over death and evil,
your triumph over darkness and despair,
your defeat of all that would deny your love and frustrate your purpose.
For the joy you have brought us –
the assurance of new life, now and for all eternity –
we worship and adore you.
Amen.

2

It was like a bolt from the blue

The other Mary

After the sabbath, as the first day of the week was dawning, Mary Magdalene and the other Mary went to see the tomb. And suddenly there was a great earthquake; for an angel of the Lord, descending from heaven, came and rolled back the stone and sat on it. His appearance was like lightning, and his clothing white as snow.

Matthew 28:1–3

Meditation

It was a bolt from the blue . . .
literally . . .
shattering the peace of the garden
and breaking in rudely on our grief.
We'd walked there in silence,
each wrapped up in our thoughts,
remembering all the special things Jesus had said and done,
precious moments neither of us would ever forget
but that had been so cruelly snatched from us
as they nailed him on a cross.
Both of us were fighting back the tears,
struggling to be strong for the sake of the other,
but as we approached the tomb we could feel ourselves crumbling,
great sobs welling up within,
and we'd have caved in completely
had it not been for that astonishing turn of events.
Suddenly,
without any warning,
any clue as to what was about to happen,
the ground seemed to shake and lightning fill the sky,
as though heaven itself was breaking in upon us.
And so, of course, it was to prove,
in a way more wonderful that we could have dared imagine.
In that awesome, earth-shattering moment, God was at work,

transforming the world for ever;
not only us but everyone,
not only life but death.
For Jesus had risen,
victorious over evil,
triumphant over the grave.
The tomb was empty,
and he was alive once more,
waiting to meet and greet us,
to speak his word again and walk with us on our way.
And this time, whatever might be,
there would be no separating us from his love,
no tearing us apart –
for we knew that, through his Spirit,
he would be with us always, to the very end of time.

Prayer

Almighty God,
we remember with awe the first Easter morning,
marvelling that, at a time when you seemed absent,
you were supremely at work,
and at a place where death seemed triumphant,
new life was coming to birth.
Remind us, should we ever forget,
that you are a God of surprises,
a God who turns the expectations of this world upside down,
bringing hope out of despair,
laughter out of tears,
light out of darkness
and life out of death.
In that knowledge, may we never despair of any situation,
no matter how bleak or hopeless things may seem.
Help us always to keep faith in your transforming power –
able to make us and all things new.
Amen.

3

The stone was rolled away

Salome

When they looked up, they saw that the stone, which was very large, had already been rolled back.

Mark 16:4

Meditation

The stone was rolled away.
I'd no idea how,
let alone what it meant,
but we saw it for ourselves,
pushed to one side,
the tomb gaping open,
almost inviting us to go inside.
And I can't tell you the relief we felt.
We'd been asking each other as we walked, 'How will we possibly get in?'
knowing we'd never move the stone ourselves,
not after watching it being rolled into place –
grown men sweating with the exertion.
But we'd gone anyway,
desperate for something to do;
to find some way of expressing our grief,
paying our last respects.
A last look at the man we'd loved so much, that's what we expected;
a final anointing with the attention he deserved.
But what a shock we had.
It was Mary, I think, who went in first,
and I could tell at once
from the way she stopped and gasped
that something was wrong,
but I still wasn't prepared for what I saw,
or rather what I *didn't* see.
For he was gone,
disappeared,
just the folded grave clothes left to mark where they had laid him.

We were speechless,
all of us,
overcome with disbelief,
not knowing what to think or do.
And then this man appeared –
don't ask me who he was –
asking what we were looking for,
as if that wasn't obvious;
and telling us to seek the living,
not the dead.
Well, we were stunned, you can imagine;
it was all such a shock,
so unexpected,
and we stood for ages,
simply nodding,
grinning,
trying to hide our embarrassment,
stop our hands from shaking.
But we went eventually,
on to Galilee as instructed;
the apostles too, once they'd got over their disbelief.
And we met him,
just as we'd been told –
Jesus!
Risen!
Alive!
Victorious!
The stone was rolled away, and I still don't know how,
but I know now what it means –
thank God, I know!

Prayer

Living God,
we praise you for the wonder of Easter –
this day of celebration, wonder and thanksgiving
that changes the way we think,
the way we act,
the way we live:
that changes everything!

We rejoice in the victory of Christ,
his triumph over evil, hatred, despair, and even death itself.
For the triumph you have won through him,
the assurance that nothing in life or death can separate us from your love;
receive our glad thanksgiving.
Amen.

4

You'd have thought we'd be pleased, wouldn't you?

Salome

So they went out and fled from the tomb, for terror and amazement had seized them; and they said nothing to anyone, for they were afraid.

Mark 16:8

Meditation

You'd have thought we'd be pleased, wouldn't you? –
over the moon at the news that he'd risen.
And we were, later,
once we finally took it all in.
But at the time it wasn't pleasure we felt,
it was sheer, unadulterated fear.
Can you blame us?
I don't think so,
for it's not every day you find a tomb empty, is it? –
not often that you go to anoint a body
only to find it's disappeared!
Yet that's what happened to us –
early that morning,
the dew still wet on the grass,
mist still rising,
the three of us making our way to the tomb,
suspecting nothing,
expecting nothing,
simply going to pay our last respects.
It was shock enough finding the stone rolled away,
our stomachs lurching at the sight of it,
and when we finally plucked up the courage to look inside,
to find not Jesus but a man we didn't know from Adam,
well, we could scarcely suppress a scream!
Who was he?

Why was he there?
What did he want?
And, most important of all, where had he taken our Lord?
The questions crowded in upon us,
our minds reeling in confusion.
He may have been calm
but *we* weren't!
We felt faint with disbelief,
dizziness growing by the second,
wanting only to get out and as far away as possible;
so when he told us to go back to the disciples,
believe me, we were only too happy to oblige.
Did we tell them what we'd seen?
Well, what do you think? Would *you* have done?
We knew all too well the response we'd get,
our words dismissed as so much nonsense –
and that's just what happened
when they finally forced it out of us,
for, try as we might, we simply couldn't hide our confusion.
We weren't just scared,
we were terrified,
trembling as though we'd seen a ghost,
and with good reason,
for we honestly thought we *had*!

Prayer

Lord Jesus Christ,
we forget sometimes the sheer wonder of your resurrection.
We've heard the accounts so often that we fail to appreciate
the enormity of what took place and the effect it had.
You were dead and buried, your body sealed in a tomb,
and for your followers that was it,
the end of a glorious dream.
When the women went to anoint your body
they expected nothing more than to perform that last act of love.
But the tomb was found empty, your body gone,
discarded grave clothes the only sign you had been laid there –
and for a time it was too much to take in.
The women returned in shock;
Mary broke down in tears;

the apostles laughed in derision,
for by all human reckoning it simply could not be.
Only it was!
You had broken the hold of death,
turned the world upside down,
transformed the course of history in one magnificent moment!
Lord Jesus Christ, as we celebrate today your victory over death
give us that same sense of awe and wonder
felt by those who first learnt the truth.
Come alive in our hearts,
so that *our* minds too will reel in wonder,
and *our* spirits dance in joyous celebration,
to the glory of your name.
Amen.

5

We thought he'd gone for ever

Mary Magdalene

Early on the first day of the week, while it was still dark, Mary Magdalene came to the tomb and saw that the stone had been removed from the tomb. So she ran and went to Simon Peter and the other disciple, the one whom Jesus loved, and said to them, 'They have taken the Lord out of the tomb, and we do not know where they have laid him.'

John 20:1, 2

Meditation

We thought he'd gone for ever,
that he'd been taken from us never to return,
for we'd seen Jesus breathe his last,
watched as they hauled him from the cross
and laid him in the tomb.
He was dead,
no doubt about it,
and we were all devastated,
overwhelmed by a tide of despair,
like ships at sea without an anchor.
What would have become of us, I wonder?
Perhaps we'd have drifted back to our old way of life,
carried on as best we could,
but I'm not sure we'd have managed it,
for we were broken,
empty,
the void too big to fill.
Thankfully, it didn't come to that,
for when we reached the tomb we found,
not a cold, lifeless corpse,
but the stone rolled away,
the grave clothes lying there, but no body!
He was risen,
alive!

We thought he'd gone,
and so he *had*,
but not as we imagined.
He'd gone *ahead* of us,
a light for our path and lamp to our feet.
He'd faced the darkness of death,
and opened the way to life.
Seen or unseen,
we know now that he's always there,
ahead of us still,
leading us safely forward,
in this world and the next,
to our journey's end.

Prayer

Living God,
we praise you that the gospel speaks not just of what you've *done*,
but also of what you're *doing*,
not simply of the resurrection of Jesus long ago,
but equally, and all the more so, of his risen life now
and the new life he offers us in turn.
Thank you for the way, through him,
you are able to transform every moment,
bringing joy out of sorrow and hope out of despair.
And thank you for the knowledge that,
whatever life may bring,
you are with us, through your Spirit,
to lead us forward from darkness into light.
Teach us to put our trust wholly in you,
confident that, come wind or rain, sunshine or shadow,
you will be there by our side,
now and always.
Amen.

6

They're not going to listen

Mary Magdalene

Now after he rose early on the first day of the week, he appeared first to Mary Magdalene, from whom he had cast out seven demons. She went out and told those who had been with him, while they were mourning and weeping.

Mark 16:9, 10

Meditation

They're not going to listen,
I can tell you that now.
They've been suspicious of me right from the start,
wondering what Jesus was thinking of
getting mixed up with someone like me.
I know what they'll say, mark my words –
that I'm making it all up;
wanting to be the centre of attention as usual;
a lovesick fool.
Not that I can blame them;
it didn't do his cause any good, after all, when I came along.
A few tax-collectors those Pharisees could stomach,
but me, I really put the cat among the pigeons.
Maybe I should have stayed away,
kept my distance,
but I loved him.
No, not in the sense they meant with their sly innuendo,
but deeper,
with everything I am,
everything I've got,
in a way that I've never loved before.
Yet not even the disciples really trusted me,
each of them finding it hard to forgive what I'd been.
And I can understand that –
for, let's face it,

I'm finding it just as hard to forgive them, for their mistakes,
their failing him when he needed them most.
But what I hold on to is those words from the cross:
'Father, forgive them, for they do not know what they do.'
He understood we all fail him,
that every one of us is unworthy,
imperfect,
yet he forgave and loved us despite that.
I thought I'd lost him,
the only one who ever truly accepted me,
and I was reconciled to struggling on alone,
no one to understand,
no one to offer their support.
But I was wrong, for he came to me.
There in the garden, overwhelmed as I was by grief,
he came to me, and hope was born again.
Not that I could believe it at first.
The voice was familiar,
the face,
the eyes,
but I told myself it couldn't be,
that it had to be the gardener,
anyone but Jesus.
And they'll do the same, I'm sure of it,
tell me I got it wrong,
that I'm overwrought,
ready to believe anything.
They won't listen, I can tell you that now,
but then I'm used to that, aren't I?
And it doesn't matter any more,
for he's accepted me
as he's accepted them,
as he accepts everyone who's ready to respond to his love
and receive his forgiveness.

Prayer

Loving God,
we thank you for the great victory we celebrate at Easter –
your triumph through Christ over evil, hatred, darkness and death,
and the assurance this gives of new life and forgiveness.
So now we acknowledge our faults,
our weakness,
and our faithlessness,
confident of your love and certain of your redeeming power.
Forgive,
renew,
restore,
by his grace.
Amen.

7

It seemed too good to be true

Peter

Now after he rose early on the first day of the week, he appeared first to Mary Magdalene, from whom he had cast out seven demons. She went out and told those who had been with him, while they were mourning and weeping. But when they heard that he was alive and had been seen by her, they would not believe it.

Mark 16:9–11

Meditation

It seemed too good to be true,
too wonderful even to contemplate he might be alive again –
so when Mary shared the news we shook our heads,
raised our eyebrows,
and laughed between our tears.
We wanted to believe it, of course we did,
more than anything else in the world,
but how could we after all we'd seen,
everything we'd been through?
Oh, it's all right for *you* –
anyone can be wise after the event –
but put yourself in our shoes;
imagine what it must have been like
having seen Jesus die as we did,
and then ask yourself honestly:
would you have felt any different?
Our faith was in tatters,
life seeming an empty void,
for how could God have let it happen,
allowed a man like that to endure such a terrible end?
Yet he had,
and we just couldn't get that knowledge out of our minds.
It had been different when Jesus was with us –
we'd looked forward then,

confident,
full of hope,
no promise too wonderful to find fulfilment;
for in those few short years of his ministry
he'd shown us another way –
the way of love, goodness, mercy –
and we'd actually believed
such things could finally triumph over evil,
no matter how impossible it seemed.
Not any more, though.
It was back to the cold harsh world of reality
where hopes are dashed and dreams lie broken,
where goodness is trampled underfoot
and love tossed back in your face,
and this time we were resolved
to keep our feet firmly on the ground,
the thought of another disappointment, another let-down,
being too much to bear.
And yet, despite it all, I had to be sure,
that flicker of hope their words had kindled
needing to be either fanned into life or laid to rest once and for all;
so I ran to the tomb, scarcely knowing what I did,
and found the stone rolled away just as they had said,
the grave clothes cast aside,
the tomb, empty!
Can it really be,
our Lord risen, alive?
I want to believe it so much,
more than you'll ever know,
but dare I take the risk of faith again?
What do *you* think –
is it too good to be true?

Prayer

Sovereign God,
in a world where evil so often triumphs
and good is tossed casually aside,
where hatred is rampant and love taken advantage of,
it is difficult not to become cynical.
The cutting edge of our faith is remorselessly blunted

by the blows life deals it,
to the point that, though we may continue to say the right words,
in our hearts we no longer believe them.
We must live in the real world, so we are told;
and as we reluctantly come to accept that,
so we lose sight of the kingdom of heaven
and our ability to trust in your transforming power.
Rekindle our faith through the testimony of Easter
to all you have done and are yet able to do.
Assure us, through experiencing again
the presence of the risen Christ in our hearts,
that with you nothing is too good to be true,
for you are able to do more than we could ever ask
or even imagine.
To you be praise and glory, now and for evermore.
Amen.

8

They said he was alive!

Peter, James and John

Now it was Mary Magdalene, Joanna, Mary the mother of James, and the other women with them who told this to the apostles. But these words seemed to them an idle tale, and they did not believe them.

Luke 24:10, 11

Meditation

Peter They said he was alive!
Can you believe that?
John All right, I know they were upset,
cut up about what had happened.
James But then, we all were, each one of us.
Peter We'd all loved him,
John all believed he was someone special,
James all hoped he was the one we were waiting for.
Peter And we were crushed by what had happened,
utterly devastated.
John We understood how the ladies felt.
Peter But you have to face facts, don't you?
John It's no good burying your head in the sand
and pretending the worst hasn't happened.
James No point trying to fool yourself
when you know the truth full well.
Peter And we knew, believe me.
John We'd seen him crying out in agony.
James We'd heard him draw his last breath.
Peter And we'd been there when they laid him in the tomb.
James At a distance, true –
keeping well out of sight, just in case.
John But he was dead, no question about it.
Peter So what were they playing at, claiming he's alive?
John They didn't seriously expect any of us to swallow it, surely?
Peter I guess they'd finally gone over the edge, lost their marbles?

James Women! We might have guessed they'd go under in a crisis.
John No wonder Jesus stuck to men for his disciples –
Peter clear-headed,
James realistic,
John down to earth,
James sensible.
Peter Jesus alive! We'd like to believe it, of course we would.
John But it's nonsense, any fool can see that.

Prayer

Lord Jesus Christ,
when we read about your resurrection sometimes,
like the first disciples we feel it's almost too good to be true.
We want to believe it, but are afraid to do so,
afraid it may all be wishful thinking.
But, again like those first disciples,
we have experienced your risen power
and been confronted by your living presence –
we know the truth of resurrection
not because we've been told about it
but because we know you by our side,
here and now,
for ourselves.
Lord Jesus Christ, we have news to share.
Help us to share it!
Amen.

9

Amazed?

Peter

But Peter got up and ran to the tomb; stooping and looking in, he saw the linen cloths by themselves; then he went home, amazed at what had happened.

Luke 24:12

Meditation

Amazed?
Is that how they tell you I felt?
Well, that's one word for it, I suppose.
I'd put it differently:
astounded,
flabbergasted,
staggered beyond words.
He was dead remember,
his body taken down from the cross and sealed in a tomb,
and every one of us had been convinced it was over,
our hopes and dreams laid to rest.
Yes, we'd seen him raise others, it's true,
but that was different:
who could raise *him*?
No point pretending, we thought,
our Lord had gone
and we were on our own.
So when the women came back from the garden,
all excitement and confusion,
I was like the others at first,
dismissing their words as idle fantasy.
It was only slowly,
as they pressed their case,
that those words of Jesus came back:
about dying and rising again,
death itself conquered.

Could it be true, I wondered?
Surely not!
And I was torn between a desire to run and see . . .
and the urge to run away.
I chose the first finally,
for I *had* to know,
just in case,
and incredibly it was all just as they had said:
the stone rolled away,
the grave clothes discarded,
the tomb empty.
He'd been dead,
no doubt about that.
But now,
marvellously,
gloriously,
he was alive!
No doubt about that either!

Prayer

Lord, we rejoice in the wonder of this day,
the awesome, amazing truth that you rose from the tomb,
conquering death and defeating evil.
We celebrate your appearing to your disciples
and your presence with us now –
the way you have walked and talked with your people
across the centuries,
kindling faith,
sharing love
and inspiring service.
Receive our joyful praise for all you have given:
life now
and life to come.
Amen.

10

One look, that's all it took!

The Apostle John

Then Peter and the other disciple set out and went towards the tomb. The two were running together, but the other disciple outran Peter and reached the tomb first. He bent down to look in and saw the linen wrappings lying there, but he did not go in. Then Simon Peter came, following him, and went into the tomb. He saw the linen wrappings lying there, and the cloth that had been on Jesus' head, not lying with the linen wrappings but rolled up in a place by itself. Then the other disciple, who reached the tomb first, also went in, and he saw and believed.

John 20:3–8

Meditation

One look, that's all it took!
One look,
and I knew beyond all doubt that God was at work,
that Jesus was alive!
I should have known it sooner, of course,
for he'd told us what to expect often enough,
but when the hammer blow fell
we simply couldn't see beyond it,
tears blinding our minds as well as our eyes.
It was when Mary came bursting in,
beside herself with excitement,
that the mist started to clear,
his words about death and resurrection flooding back
and rekindling a flame that had all but been extinguished.
I ran then as I've never run before,
hope lending wings to my feet,
heart pounding within me,
not just from the exertion
but from the emotion that had taken hold of me,
the curious mixture of fear and exhilaration.

I wanted so much to believe it was true,
only I was afraid it might be some cruel hoax
or fancy of the imagination,
a trick of the mind or, worse still, of our enemies.
But when I went in to the tomb
and found the abandoned grave clothes,
then I knew,
and my spirit soared in jubilation.
He was not there:
he had risen just as he promised,
death not able to have the final word.
And suddenly everything fitted into place,
the heartache, the hurt, the humiliation –
it was all meant to be,
all a part of God's sovereign purpose!
Where we had seen darkness, he had brought light!
Where there had been death, now there was life!
Everything was turned around,
transformed,
renewed,
sharing in the wonder of resurrection.
One look, that's all it took –
one look, and life was changed for ever!

Prayer

Gracious God,
we thank you that our faith
is not founded on theory or speculation –
on the ideas of theologians or the musings of philosophers –
but is rooted in the living testimony of ordinary people like us,
the testimony of countless generations of believers
who have encountered the risen Christ for themselves
through his Spirit.
In him, you came, lived, died and rose again,
making yourself known through the concrete events of history.
For all who saw for themselves and passed the message on,
receive our thanks.

And for all that we experience today
of your continuing love and life-giving purpose,
we give you our praise in joyful worship,
through Jesus Christ, our risen, victorious Saviour.
Amen.

11

I was shattered at the time

Mary Magdalene

But Mary stood weeping outside the tomb.

John 20:11a

Meditation

I was shattered at the time,
inconsolable.
It was as though the bottom had fallen out of my world
and there was nothing left to live for.
How could they do that to him, I asked myself?
How could they destroy someone so loving and gentle,
so caring,
so good?
Yet they had.
I'd seen it for myself,
watched as he drew his last agonised breath;
and it was dreadful,
more terrible than I can ever describe.
It wasn't just the pain he went through, though that was awful enough;
it was the isolation of it all –
standing there before Pilate, alone,
forsaken by his friends,
one man against the might of an empire;
groaning under the lash of the whip, alone,
no one to offer him comfort or bathe his wounds;
hanging upon that cross, alone,
crying out in such heart-breaking anguish,
as though he were separated not just from us but from God himself.
I felt at the time I would never forget it,
that the memory would haunt me for the rest of my days.
And so it would have done,
unquestionably,
were it not for what came after.

It was all so unexpected –
suddenly, in the nightmare of my grief, a ray of sunshine,
and then joy, immersing me in its light.
One moment despair,
then the stone rolled away,
the tomb empty,
the mysterious stranger appearing from nowhere,
and that familiar voice speaking my name.
One moment tears,
the next laughter.
One moment death,
the next life.
And now my heart dances with delight.
I still can scarcely take it in though,
having to pinch myself sometimes to be sure it's not all a dream.
But no, it's true.
He died yet rose again;
was killed but conquered death;
lived and lives again!
I truly thought life was over,
not just for him but for me.
But I was wrong, wasn't I?
For it wasn't over;
it was only just beginning.

Prayer

Gracious God,
thank you that you have always been with us,
in the bad times as well as the good,
the difficult as well as the easy,
the sad as well as the happy.
Thank you that when we have been uncertain of the way ahead,
you have given us guidance;
when we have felt discouraged,
you have given us fresh inspiration;
when we have been in despair,
you have given us hope.
Thank you for the assurance Easter brings
of your steadfast love that never ceases,
of your mercies new every morning,

of your great faithfulness.
Give us that confidence in the days ahead,
so that whatever problems we may face,
whatever disappointments we may experience,
whatever sorrows may befall us,
we shall still find reason to look forward,
reason to believe in the future,
and reason to hope.
Amen.

12

I was distraught

Mary Magdalene

As she wept, she bent over to look into the tomb; and she saw two angels in white, sitting where the body of Jesus had been lying, one at the head and the other at the feet. They said to her, 'Woman, why are you weeping?' She said to them, 'They have taken away my Lord, and I do not know where they have laid him.' When she had said this, she turned round and saw Jesus standing there, but she did not know that it was Jesus.

John 20:11b–14

Meditation

I was distraught,
eyes blinded by grief,
heart numb with sorrow,
for I honestly believed they'd taken away his body
and I'd never see Jesus again.
All right, he was dead,
so what does it matter, you say?
But it did to me,
for I wanted to pay my respects,
to gaze on that gentle face,
that lovely man,
just one more time.
I wanted to remember him at peace,
not groaning on a cross;
to see him laid to rest
and know his suffering was truly over.
And now, it seemed, I was to be denied even that,
his corpse stolen like some grisly trophy,
my dearest friend pursued to the last by his enemies.
It all but finished me,
and I broke down in tears,
conscious of nothing and no one but my grief.
Not even those strangers in the tomb could shake me from it –

my only thought being that someone had taken away my Lord,
and I'd no idea where they'd laid him.
No point looking, I thought –
he was gone,
lost to us for ever.
But I was wrong –
wonderfully, gloriously wrong –
for I'd no need to find him at all:
he found *me*!

Prayer

Risen Lord,
with hearts ablaze,
filled with praise and wonder,
we celebrate the truth that death is not the end;
that you rose from the grave,
opening the way to life for all.
With a song on our lips,
heartfelt hymns of joy and thanksgiving,
we celebrate the fact that love is stronger than hatred,
good greater than evil,
and light mightier than darkness.
With laughter in our eyes,
sparkling with faith and hope,
we celebrate the proof that sorrow will turn to joy,
hurt to wholeness
and defeat to victory.
With gratitude deep within,
filling body, mind and spirit,
we celebrate the assurance that your kingdom will never end,
your purpose never fail
your love never fade
and your mercy never be exhausted.
Gladly, we worship you.
Amen.

13

We met him, there on the Emmaus road

Cleopas

Now on that same day two of them were going to a village called Emmaus, about seven miles from Jerusalem, and talking with each other about all these things that had happened. While they were talking and discussing, Jesus himself came near and went with them, but their eyes were kept from recognising him. And he said to them, 'What are you discussing with each other while you walk along?' They stood still, looking sad. Then one of them, whose name was Cleopas, answered him, 'Are you the only stranger in Jerusalem who does not know the things that have taken place there in these days?'

Luke 24:13–18

Meditation

We met him, there on the Emmaus road,
and still we didn't understand –
can you believe that?
Despite the testimony of the women and the apostles,
the empty tomb,
the vision of angels,
still we couldn't take it in!
I suppose we'd made up our minds that it was finished,
come to terms with the fact that our hopes had been dashed,
and we just couldn't bring ourselves to think any different
for fear of yet more disappointment,
yet more broken dreams.
Condemn us, if you like,
but remember this:
we'd seen him hanging there on the cross,
contorted in agony,
we'd watched in desolation as he drew his final breath,
and we'd been there, tears streaming from our eyes,
as they cut him down and laid him in the tomb.
You don't forget that in a hurry, I can tell you.

So when this stranger appeared out of the blue
we thought nothing of it –
why should we? –
the possibility of him being Jesus was the last thing on our minds.
Even when he interpreted the Scriptures for us,
explaining why the Messiah had to suffer and die,
still we didn't suspect anything –
despite our hearts burning within us with inexplicable joy.
But when we sat together at table,
and he took bread and broke it,
then even *we* couldn't miss it,
the extraordinary, incredible truth –
it *was* Jesus,
Christ crucified and risen,
there by our sides!
We'd thought the adventure was over,
but it had only just begun.
We'd assumed there was nothing left to us but memories,
but suddenly the future beckoned, rich with promise.
The night had ended,
a new day was dawning,
life was beginning again –
and we marvelled at the sheer wonder of his grace,
for, of course, *we* didn't meet *him* that day,
despite what we'd thought;
he met *us*!

Prayer

Lord Jesus Christ,
you speak your word to us
as you spoke it to the apostles long ago:
'Come, follow me.'
You call us as you have called so many over the years:
'Come to me, all you that are weary
and are carrying heavy burdens,
and I will give you rest.'
You offer us, as you offer all your people,
refreshment for our souls:
'Let anyone who is thirsty come to me,
and let the one who believes in me drink.'

Lord, we thank you for such invitations,
and gladly we respond.
But, more than that, we thank you
for the fact that before anyone comes to you,
you come first to them.
You came to Peter, James and John by the lakeside;
to the hungry, the sick and the outcasts in the streets of Galilee;
to Mary Magdalene weeping in the garden;
to two weary disciples walking the Emmaus road;
to the apostles trembling behind locked doors;
to Saul breathing murder on the road to Damascus;
and so to countless others since.
Always it is you who makes the first approach,
calling your people to faith,
and still you come through your Spirit to meet with us.
Open our eyes to your presence
and lead us forward in your service
until that day when, with all your people,
we enter your kingdom and meet you face to face.
Amen.

14

So that's who it was!

Cleopas

When he was at the table with them, he took bread, blessed and broke it, and gave it to them. Then their eyes were opened, and they recognised him; and he vanished from their sight.

Luke 24:30, 31

Meditation

So that's who it was!
I see it now, staring me in the face.
But how could we have not realised it before?
That's what I don't understand.
You see, we'd been to Jerusalem,
watched with our own eyes what they did to him,
even stood at the foot of the cross,
yet we didn't recognise him when he walked beside us.
Why?
Was it sorrow that blinded us,
our hearts too full of grief to glimpse the truth?
It's possible, for we were devastated, there's no denying that.
We'd thought he was the one we longed for,
coming to redeem our people,
and it had been a terrible blow after arriving full of hope,
anticipating his kingdom,
to see him nailed to that cross,
bruised and broken,
the life seeping from his bleeding body.
We'd been so certain,
so sure he was the Messiah,
but we'd seen his death
and were making our way back home,
our dreams in tatters,
our lives in ruins.
That could have clouded our eyes, unquestionably,

for we had little time after such a disappointment
for anything or anyone.
He was the last person we expected to meet, I can tell you that.
Oh, I know he'd talked of rising again,
returning from the grave –
we were talking of it even as we walked –
but we'd taken it all with a pinch of salt,
and in our hearts we'd given him up,
reluctantly making our way back to reality.
We never imagined for a moment we might see him;
the thought simply never entered our heads.
So yes, perhaps that explains it,
why for all the time he was with us the penny failed to drop.
Yet it was more than that,
for it wasn't finally his face we recognised.
It went far deeper –
the way he spoke,
the way he acted,
the way our hearts burned within us as we walked,
and, above all, the meal that we shared.
He took bread,
and broke it,
and suddenly we realised, with a certainty nothing could shake,
that he was Jesus,
risen,
alive,
victorious.
Yet, even as we saw it, he disappeared,
vanishing before our eyes,
and we've never seen him since.
It's funny that, isn't it? –
how we saw him most clearly when we couldn't see him at all,
how our eyes were opened when we weren't even looking,
and how we know he's with us now,
even though he's departed from our side!

Prayer

Lord Jesus Christ,
like the two disciples on the Emmaus road,
so often we journey through life unaware of your presence.
Though we talk of your resurrection
it does not stir our hearts or capture our imagination
in the way it should.
Yet though we may not realise it,
even in our doubt you are there with us,
matching your stride to ours,
waiting to meet us along the way.
Open our eyes
so that we may see and know you better.
Amen.

15

We were returning to Emmaus

Cleopas

They said to each other, 'Were not our hearts burning within us while he was talking to us on the road, while he was opening the scriptures to us?' That same hour they got up and returned to Jerusalem; and they found the eleven and their companions gathered together. They were saying, 'The Lord has risen indeed, and he has appeared to Simon!' Then they told what had happened on the road, and how he had been made known to them in the breaking of the bread.

Luke 24:32–35

Meditation

We were returning to Emmaus,
heading back the way we'd come,
but in truth we were going nowhere,
life suddenly empty,
devoid of direction,
for they'd crucified Jesus,
the one on whom we'd pinned our hopes.
We'd thought him the Messiah,
the promised one of God who'd set us free,
and when he'd ridden into Jerusalem acclaimed like a king
we'd assumed the time had come:
the moment when he'd take up his throne and start to rule.
But now he was dead,
and with him had gone our faith in the future,
our faith in *anything*.
What sort of God would let that happen?
Why hadn't he intervened?
We tried to make sense of it as we talked together,
but there too we trod the same old ground –
one step forward and the next backwards.
Until, that is, this stranger met us and walked by our side.
Until we broke bread and shared wine.

Until he opened the Scriptures and unfolded their meaning.
Then, suddenly, we knew the truth.
It was Jesus –
risen,
victorious,
alive!
That's why God let it happen.
He *had* intervened, right there on the cross!
And though Jesus vanished even as the truth dawned,
we knew somehow he'd be with us always,
the King of kings and Lord of lords.
We set off again,
resuming our journey,
but this time we were no longer going nowhere:
we were walking the way of Christ!

Prayer

Risen Lord,
remind us that, with you by our sides,
faith should be an ongoing journey,
an unfolding story of adventure and discovery.
Give us an expectation of new experiences and insights,
an openness to new horizons,
a desire to grow in grace, wisdom and commitment.
Reveal your presence to us through your word,
your world,
your Church,
your Spirit,
and help us to greet each day in the knowledge that you are with us,
leading us forward,
whatever we face,
in life or in death –
each moment being another step on the road
to the joys you hold in store,
now and for evermore.
Amen.

16

It wasn't just the *doors* that were locked

The Apostle James

When it was evening on that day, the first day of the week, and the doors of the house where the disciples had met were locked for fear of the Jews, Jesus came and stood among them and said, 'Peace be with you.' After he said this, he showed them his hands and his side. Then the disciples rejoiced when they saw the Lord.

John 20:19, 20

Meditation

It wasn't just the *doors* that were locked –
it was our hearts as well,
shut tight against the world,
the future
and the truth.
We were terrified that the Pharisees would come for us
as they'd come so recently for Jesus;
that they'd do to us what they'd done to him.
We dreaded what lay ahead,
convinced that, without Jesus, we could never cope.
And yes,
though faith should have stirred again within us
after those reports of the empty tomb,
the stone rolled aside,
the Lord risen,
still we couldn't quite accept it,
none of us daring to believe
in case it were some cruel delusion.
So we sat there,
too shocked to face the past,
too shaken to trust the future,
too shattered to live in the present,
each of us imprisoned by fear, grief and doubt.
Until, that is,

as so often before,
Jesus stood among us!
He was alive,
victorious,
by our side once more!
No door could keep him out.
No grave could keep him in.
And suddenly our hearts were open,
set free to live again.
Whatever had been,
whatever was,
whatever would be,
Jesus was there too.
What more did we need to know!

Prayer

Whatever our worries in the present,
whatever our fears for the future,
teach us, Lord, to trust in you,
assured that, in life or in death,
your love is stronger than all.
Help us to live each day,
each moment,
in that sure and certain faith.
Amen.

17

He was back!

Peter

Later he appeared to the eleven themselves as they were sitting at the table; and he upbraided them for their lack of faith and stubbornness, because they had not believed those who saw him after he had risen.

Mark 16:14

Meditation

He was back!
Back in the land of the living,
just when we'd given up hope!
Three days it had been,
three days of dark despair as slowly the truth sank home:
our Lord, laid in a tomb,
dead and buried,
never to walk this earth again.
We couldn't believe it at first,
none of us,
even though we'd seen it for ourselves.
We expected to wake up any moment
to find it was all some horrible nightmare,
a dreadful mistake that had somehow taken us in.
But as the numbness passed, so the reality hit us,
and the pain began in earnest.
It was an end to everything –
our plans,
our hopes,
our dreams.
There was nothing left to live for,
that's how we felt –
we'd pinned our hopes on him,
and he was gone.
Only he wasn't!
He was there,

meeting Mary in the garden as her heart broke beside the tomb.
He was there,
on the Emmaus road as two followers trudged slowly home,
their world in tatters.
He was there,
speaking to Thomas, breaking through his disbelief!
He was there,
standing among us in the upper room!
He was back in the land of the living,
and suddenly so were we –
faith rekindled,
hope renewed,
joy reborn,
life beginning again!

Prayer

Lord Jesus Christ,
just when it looked all over,
when the world had written you off
and even your disciples had given up on you,
you came back – defeat revealed as victory.
Teach us what that means for us today:
not only the promise of life to come,
but good news for life here and now.
Help us to understand that, whatever tragedies we may suffer,
obstacles face,
or disappointments experience,
we can bounce back from them with your help,
for you are a God able to transform even the darkest moments
and lead us through them into the light of your love.
Gladly, then, we put our hand in yours,
knowing that in life or in death
you will never fail or forsake us.
Amen.

18

We've seen Jesus!

Andrew

When it was evening on that day, the first day of the week, and the doors of the house where the disciples had met were locked for fear of the Jews, Jesus came and stood among them and said, 'Peace be with you.' After he said this, he showed them his hands and his side. Then the disciples rejoiced when they saw the Lord.

John 20:19, 20

Meditation

We've seen Jesus!
No, don't laugh,
we've seen him, I tell you!
We made the mistake of dismissing it ourselves,
scoffing when the women came racing back wild-eyed with excitement.
'Pull yourselves together!' we told them,
'For God's sake calm down!'
We couldn't believe he was alive,
refused to accept it could possibly be true.
And when they admitted they couldn't be certain,
that they'd only seen the empty tomb rather than Jesus himself,
then we looked for some simpler explanation,
an answer more in line with common sense.
Even when Mary returned, tears of joy in her eyes,
when the two from Emmaus spoke of having seen him,
we wouldn't accept it, certain that we knew best.
It's understandable, I suppose;
I mean, you'd think twice, wouldn't you,
if you'd seen your best friend murdered,
sealed in the tomb,
only to be told he'd been spotted down the street?
And anyway, we didn't want to build our hopes up.
We were still reeling from the shock, the horror, the sorrow of it all.
Yet, if I'm honest, there's more to it than that,

for, most of all, our pride was hurt.
If he was alive, we reasoned, then why hadn't we seen him?
Why should Mary,
or those two disciples,
or anyone else come to that,
have met him before we did?
We were his chosen disciples,
the ones who'd given up everything to follow him,
taken all the risks –
so if Jesus had risen, surely we'd have known?
It's awful, I know, but that's the way we saw it
until he finally appeared to us.
We should have remembered, of course, what he'd said so often,
about how the first will be last,
the least greatest,
but we still had much to learn
and were too full of ourselves by half.
Anyway, there we were,
huddled together in that upstairs room,
arguing about what it all meant,
when there *he* was too,
standing among us,
arms outstretched in welcome.
Where he came from or went afterwards I've no idea.
I only know that it was him –
Jesus –
and that he was alive:
wonderfully,
amazingly,
gloriously,
alive!

Prayer

Loving God,
despite our faith we have to confess there are times
when we find life difficult,
when situations seem hopeless,
when we look to the future fearfully
wondering what good it can possibly hold.
Help us to understand that the truth of resurrection

is not just limited to the future,
to life after death,
but is about the present,
life now!
Help us to realise it speaks not just about eternal issues
but about our daily lives –
the mundane and routine.
Help us to understand that even there,
and especially there,
you bring resurrection.
Amen.

19

What's done cannot be undone, isn't that what they say?

Bartholomew

While in their joy they were disbelieving and still wondering, he said to them, 'Have you anything here to eat?' They gave him a piece of broiled fish, and he took it and ate in their presence.

Luke 24:41–43

Meditation

What's done cannot be undone, isn't that what they say?
As much as we might wish otherwise,
it's impossible to turn the clock back.
And that's exactly what we'd thought just a few days before,
as we stood in desolation
and watched the Master suffer on that cross;
as we watched him breathe his last;
as we saw him cut down, limp and lifeless,
and carried to the tomb.
It was over,
finished,
those three wonderful years we'd spent with him at an end,
never to be repeated.
What possible reason was there to think otherwise?
So when the women burst in on us,
babbling about the tomb being empty,
the stone rolled away,
well, I hate to say it, but we didn't pay much attention.
It just couldn't be, could it?
At least that's what the theory said;
the facts told a different story –
and what a story it was!
For the next thing we knew he was there amongst us:
the one they thought they'd destroyed, back from the grave,

he who'd been dead and buried, alive!
And in that moment the world itself was turned upside down,
for suddenly we knew beyond doubt
that what's done *can* be undone,
the proof right there, before our very eyes.
Defeat had become victory,
despair, hope,
sorrow, joy,
darkness, light,
tears, laughter!
The forces of evil had conspired to do their worst,
only for the havoc they'd wreaked
to be wiped away in a moment,
rolled back, as surely as the stone from the tomb,
by the power of love!
Do you realise what that means?
That no situation is too hopeless,
no person too dreadful,
to be beyond redemption.
That no matter who we are or what we do,
however much we fail,
however far we stray,
still he can turn us round and transform our lives.
That there is nothing in heaven or earth,
in life or death,
that can finally separate us
from the love of God revealed in Christ!
He'd been to the cross,
carried our sins,
wrestled with the powers of darkness,
and had triumphed over it all.
Life was beginning again,
for you,
for me,
for everyone willing to receive it.
That, and that alone, cannot be undone!

Prayer

Lord,
we live in a world in which nothing seems to change
yet nothing remains the same.
We look around us,
and see the same mistakes being made
as those that have littered the course of history.
We look at ourselves,
and though the appearance may have altered a little,
we see the same old person staring out at us,
beset still by familiar faults and weaknesses.
For all our hopes of progress,
all our efforts at improvement,
human nature seldom varies.
It's a depressing and frustrating thought.
And yet it is only half the story,
for in Christ you died and rose again,
and in so doing transformed the world.
Though the old lives on, the new is here,
at work in the world,
at work in our lives,
taking what is and shaping it into what shall be.
Through him we have forgiveness,
the invitation to put our former selves behind us
and to be born again,
life truly different.
Lord, though all else may change,
we know that *you* will not.
What you have done for us is done for ever!
Thanks be to God!
Amen.

20

I wanted to know, that's all

Thomas

But Thomas (who was called the Twin), one of the twelve, was not with them when Jesus came. So the other disciples told him, 'We have seen the Lord.' But he said to them, 'Unless I see the mark of the nails in his hands, and put my finger in the mark of the nails and my hand in his side, I will not believe.'

John 20:24, 25

Meditation

I wanted to know, that's all,
to see for myself if it could possibly be true.
Was that so awful of me?
Remember, we'd *all* doubted at first
when the women came back that morning,
each of us dismissing their story of the empty tomb
as so much nonsense,
so why point the finger at me,
as though *I* questioned and *they* didn't?
All right, the situation had changed since then, I accept that,
for they claimed to have seen him in the meantime,
others saying the same,
each adamant the Lord had risen,
yet much as I wanted to believe it, I simply couldn't,
not unless someone could offer conclusive proof.
That was me all over, I'm afraid,
the way I'd been since a boy,
struggling to accept anything I couldn't touch for myself
or see with my own eyes,
and I'd said as much to Jesus before he died;
that day he spoke about his Father's house,
and his going there to prepare a place for us.
'Believe in God,' he'd said,
'believe also in me.'

A wonderful promise, yes,
only to me he was talking in riddles,
and I made no bones about it:
'Lord, we do not know where you are going.
How can we know the way?'
He wasn't angry at that,
though he could have been,
for after all he'd said, I should have known what he meant,
just as I should have understood he would rise from the tomb
and return among us.
He'd spoken of it, often enough,
done his best to prepare us not simply for his death
but for his resurrection to follow,
but, as so often happens, we dwelt on the bad
and forgot the good,
unable to see beyond the horizon of the present moment.
So, despite it all, I refused to believe,
convinced there were too many questions
and not enough answers.
And I'd be doing that still,
wondering if it ever could be,
only suddenly he was there again,
standing among us,
arms outstretched in welcome,
those pierced hands reaching out to me, Thomas . . .
and I knew I'd been wrong.
He was alive, just as they'd said,
risen and victorious –
and I knelt down in worship,
my heart overflowing with thanksgiving,
for he'd come, despite me,
despite my lack of faith.
Though I had doubted him,
still he believed in me!

Prayer

Lord,
we do not always believe as we should.
We try our hardest, but our faith is weak
and we lose sight of all you have promised

and all you are able to do.
There is so much in life that is a mystery,
seeming to deny everything we believe about you.
Despite our good intentions,
doubt sometimes gets the upper hand
so that we begin to question even what is most precious to us.
Yet though we are faithless to you,
always you are faithful to us,
refusing to let us go.
Come to us now,
and help us to glimpse a little more of your glory,
so that we may confess you again,
today and every day,
as our Lord
and our God.
Amen.

21

Did he condemn me for doubting?

Thomas

A week later his disciples were again in the house, and Thomas was with them. Although the doors were shut, Jesus came and stood among them and said, 'Peace be with you.' Then he said to Thomas, 'Put your finger here and see my hands. Reach out your hand and put it in my side. Do not doubt but believe.'

John 20:26–28

Meditation

Did he condemn me for doubting?
Not a bit of it –
he understood,
and answered.
Perhaps I should have believed earlier –
after all, I had my fellow disciples' word that Jesus was alive –
but you can appreciate I wanted to be sure.
Don't forget, we were grief-stricken when he died,
numb with despair,
none of us listening when Mary and the others
rushed back from the tomb
declaring it was empty and the Lord raised –
no, not one.
We feared it was wishful thinking,
a beautiful but sad delusion,
for though Jesus had spoken of rising again,
we never imagined it could really happen.
It was just my luck not to be there when he appeared like that,
and though I longed to accept he was truly alive,
I didn't dare to trust lest it were all to prove a ghastly mistake.
I couldn't have lived with more disappointment,
not after what we'd been through already,
so I closed my mind to the idea until Jesus stood before me,
inviting me to touch, and feel, and know.

Seeing is believing,
isn't that what they say,
and so it was for me.
So how, you may ask, can anyone possibly believe without seeing?
Well actually they *can*,
for even though he's gone from us now,
returned to the Father,
I know he's with me still,
every moment of the day –
here through his Spirit in his risen power.
I can't see him,
but I can feel his presence,
for ever by my side.
Not that you have take my word for it –
I wouldn't expect that.
Respond,
and discover the truth for yourself.
Do not doubt,
but believe!

Prayer

Lord Jesus Christ,
we have faith in you –
in who and what you are,
what you mean,
what you have done
and what you will yet do.
But we also have doubts –
things we don't understand,
that we cannot make sense of,
that we struggle to accept.
Alongside our belief is unbelief,
alongside trust, uncertainty.
Accept us, we pray, despite the warring voices within.
Deepen our faith and respond to our doubts,
assuring us of your living presence and constant love.
Though we will never have *all* the answers,
teach us that in you we have the one answer we really need.
Amen.

22

Would you believe it!

Thomas

But Thomas (who was called the Twin), one of the twelve, was not with them when Jesus came. So the other disciples told him, 'We have seen the Lord.' But he said to them, 'Unless I see the mark of the nails in his hands, and put my finger in the mark of the nails and my hand in his side, I will not believe.'

John 20:24, 25

Meditation

Would you believe it!
They're all at it now, the whole daft lot of them!
I never thought I'd see the day.
Not Peter, anyway –
I thought he had more sense.
And James and John?
Hot-headed at times perhaps,
but they had their heads screwed on,
or so I thought.
Okay, maybe the others were a little suspect.
Simon for one.
To be honest, I felt like he'd believe anything sometimes.
And the rest?
They had their moments too, to put it kindly.
But this?
Jesus alive and kicking,
dropping in on them for a quiet chat . . . ?
Who are they trying to kid?
It really is beyond me.
I mean, they were the first to mock when the women came back
trembling and laughing like a bunch of mixed-up children.
We all agreed it was nothing more than hysteria, poor things.
So what's changed?
What's got into them?

If you ask me it's this cursed waiting:
waiting for the sound of footsteps,
for the knock on the door,
for the moment when we know it's all up for us
just as it was for him.
That's enough to make anyone go off their trolley.
But, even so, you won't catch me rabbiting on about Jesus being alive –
I'll want more than a few fanciful visions before I start doing that.
Let me touch him perhaps,
see the scars,
put my hand in that spear-wound,
feel where they smashed those nails home,
and then, who knows, it might be different.
But be honest, what chance is there of that?
Do you believe it could happen?
I don't.

Prayer

Lord Jesus Christ,
it's hard sometimes to believe.
In the face of frustrated hopes and broken dreams,
of sorrow, suffering and death,
we too, like Thomas, can find ourselves doubting,
wanting irrefutable proof before we dare accept what we are told.
You appeared to Thomas and gave him the assurance he wanted,
but you also told him that those who have not seen but still believe
are most blessed of all.
Help us then, even when faith is hard,
even when it's a struggle to hold on,
to put our trust in you,
knowing that you will not fail us.
Amen.

23

I feel sorry for Thomas

Matthew

Thomas answered him, 'My Lord and my God!' Jesus said to him, 'Have you believed because you have seen me? Blessed are those who have not seen and yet have come to believe.'

John 20:28, 29

Meditation

I feel sorry for Thomas,
for people talk of him in the same breath as doubt,
as if the two are synonymous,
each belonging together.
Okay, so he didn't believe at first, I'll grant you that,
but he wasn't alone:
we *all* struggled at the beginning to accept it was really him –
our friend Jesus returned to life
and standing there among us.
We'd seen him crucified, remember,
his body dragged from the cross and laid in a tomb,
limp and lifeless.
And when we'd gathered together that first day of the week,
we'd locked and bolted the doors,
scared stiff our enemies would come for us
as they'd come just days before for Jesus.
Would *you* have expected him to stroll in suddenly
as if nothing had happened?
To appear out of the blue by your side,
alive and well?
Of course not.
You'd have pinched yourself, as *we* did,
rubbed your eyes in amazement
convinced you were seeing things,
the light playing tricks with your eyes.
Not one of us believed completely

until he showed us his hands and side;
then we could see for ourselves it was true.
So don't be too hard on Thomas . . .
or on yourself . . .
for Jesus didn't condemn him any more than the rest of us.
He asks for faith,
and he'll help it to grow,
but he also understands doubt,
and will help that to *go*.

Prayer

Loving God,
when we find faith hard,
all kinds of questions forcing themselves into our minds,
all sorts of doubts arising unbidden and refusing to be quelled,
save us from hiding them away,
as if they are a guilty secret,
a weakness to be ashamed of;
and save us from pretending they aren't there –
struggling on with them unresolved.
Teach us to bring them honestly before you,
seeking your guidance and insight,
so that we may understand more of you and your ways.
Nurture our belief,
and help us to deal with our unbelief,
through Jesus Christ our Lord.
Amen.

24

I thought I'd seen a ghost

The Apostle James

While they were talking about this, Jesus himself stood among them and said to them, 'Peace be with you.' They were startled and terrified, and thought that they were seeing a ghost. He said to them, 'Why are you frightened, and why do doubts arise in your hearts? Look at my hands and my feet; see that it is I myself. Touch me and see; for a ghost does not have flesh and bones as you see that I have.'

Luke 24:36–39

Meditation

I thought I'd seen a ghost.
No joking, I really did.
Oh, I shouldn't have done, I realise that –
not after everything Jesus had said,
and certainly not after the reports we'd heard
from those who'd seen him –
but we were still struggling to take it in,
more troubled than happy at the news,
afraid that something spooky was going on.
And when suddenly he appeared, popping up out of nowhere,
I was absolutely petrified.
Well, we *all* were, let's be honest,
though we were loth to admit it publicly.
We nearly jumped out of our skins when we saw him,
and though we hurriedly composed ourselves,
trying to look as though we'd been expecting him all along,
we couldn't fool Jesus.
He'd seen our faces,
taken in our reactions at a glance,
and in his eyes I caught both surprise and disappointment.
'Why are you frightened?' he asked us.
'Why do you doubt so much?
Look and see: is it me, or isn't it?'

Yet it wasn't as simple as that,
not even after we'd seen his hands,
touched his feet,
felt his side.
We knew it was him, but we still couldn't quite believe it
despite what our eyes were telling us.
It was too good to be true, I suppose.
We were afraid to trust ourselves,
afraid it might all be wishful thinking,
a case of seeing what we wanted to see.
We didn't want to raise our hopes only to have them dashed again,
so we simply stood and gawped.
Yet there could be no denying it,
not when he ate with us,
talked with us,
laughed with us.
After that, it was almost like it had been before,
him and us together,
and we knew then that somehow,
in a way we couldn't quite understand,
he'd come back to us!
Yet it wasn't quite how it used to be –
there was something different,
something about him we couldn't quite put our finger on.
It was Jesus all right,
unquestionably the man we'd loved and followed,
and he was there by our sides, flesh and blood as we are.
But we realised that though he'd come back to us
we would have to let him go,
have to part again.
There could be no return to what had gone before,
no turning the clock back and pretending nothing had happened.
It was the end of a chapter,
a chapter we had wanted to go on for ever.
Yet it was also the beginning of another,
the turning of a new page,
with no knowing where it might lead.

Prayer

Lord Jesus Christ,
thank you for meeting us day by day,
just as you met your disciples in the days following your resurrection.
Thank you that your victory of good over evil,
love over hate
and life over death
continues to make a difference to our lives,
just as it did to theirs.
Thank you for continuing to turn weakness into strength,
fear into confidence,
and doubt into faith.
Thank you, above all, that for each of us
there is always the assurance of a new beginning
when it seems like the end,
new hope where there seems only despair.
Amen.

25

It was like the loaves and fishes all over again

Nathanael

When they had gone ashore, they saw a charcoal fire there, with fish on it, and bread. Jesus said to them, 'Bring some of the fish that you have just caught.' So Simon Peter went aboard and hauled the net ashore, full of large fish, a hundred and fifty-three of them; and though there were so many, the net was not torn. Jesus said to them, 'Come and have breakfast.' Now none of the disciples dared to ask him, 'Who are you?' because they knew it was the Lord. Jesus came and took the bread and gave it to them, and did the same with the fish.

John 21:9–13

Meditation

It was like the loaves and fishes all over again,
only this time there was no multitude to feed –
just us, a handful of disciples.
We'd been fishing all night,
and were famished,
but there seemed no prospect of food,
for, despite all our efforts,
all our skills,
we'd caught nothing.
But then, Jesus appeared,
and suddenly everything changed,
our nets,
after we let them down where he told us to,
not just full
but fit to burst.
We'd enough and more than enough,
breakfasting that day like kings!
We trawl for *people* now instead of fish,
but it's the same story,
the same lesson we need to learn.

for if the call is *ours*,
the mission is *his*.
We have a part to play,
but results are down to him.
We can do nothing,
he does all.
Never think, then, that success is down to you –
your words,
your gifts,
your ingenuity –
for you couldn't be more wrong.
Let down your nets –
lovingly,
honestly,
faithfully –
and *he* will supply the catch.

Prayer

In all you call us to do, Lord,
everything you call us to be,
remind us that we do it not in our strength
but through yours.
Teach us that what is impossible for us
is possible for you;
that what we could never hope to achieve through our own efforts
can be accomplished by your resurrection power.
Help us, then, to work for you,
speak for you,
live for you,
love for you,
confident that if we do our part,
you will do yours.
Amen.

26

We still hadn't seen it, you know

Andrew

Then he said to them, 'These are my words that I spoke to you while I was still with you – that everything written about me in the law of Moses, the prophets, and the psalms must be fulfilled.'

Luke 24:44

Meditation

We still hadn't seen it, you know,
not even after he stood there among us, alive and well.
We still imagined that his death had been a ghastly mistake,
an unforeseen catastrophe that somehow,
miraculously,
God had put right,
salvaging triumph from disaster.
Perhaps some of us had an inkling otherwise –
Peter, James and John, for example –
but not me, I'm afraid;
I was convinced he'd snatched victory from the jaws of defeat.
Only, of course, I couldn't have been more wrong,
as I learnt that day when Jesus opened the Scriptures,
and opened, along with them, our minds.
It took some doing, believe me,
for I was a slow learner,
but slowly it sunk in –
the mind-boggling truth that it was all there:
suffering,
death,
resurrection,
each foretold,
each purposed long before,
each part of God's saving plan.
I was staggered,
overwhelmed,

for it was everywhere,
the words leaping out at me from the pages –
the prophets,
the psalms,
the Law,
all pointing to him –
and I marvelled at the realisation that for so long,
so many years,
God had been building up to that one moment,
that astonishing expression of his love –
his Son on a cross!
The shadow of death had been the cradle of life,
the descent into darkness the dawning of light!
Unseen,
unnoticed,
our God had been there,
in the worst of moments as well as the best,
enfolding all in his mighty hand.
And I glimpsed for a moment the awesome truth:
that he'd brought us joy,
not despite sorrow
but through it –
the only way such joy could be.

Prayer

Sovereign God,
we are so used to clearing up after our mistakes,
making the best of a bad job,
that we can sometimes mistakenly interpret the resurrection
in those terms –
as your putting right what had gone so badly wrong
in the suffering and death of Jesus.
Yet in so doing we misunderstand the wonder of the gospel,
for at Easter we celebrate not the reversal of a disaster
but the culmination of your divine purpose
in which both death and resurrection were integral components.
Before the crown of glory there had to come the crown of thorns;
before *your* hands could raise him from the tomb,
his hands had to be pierced on the cross –
the two went together, one without the other impossible.

Teach us that it is only through giving that we receive,
through letting go that we find,
through dying to self that we shall rise to eternal life,
and, in understanding that,
may we celebrate the true wonder of Christ crucified and risen!
Amen.

27

How did we not see it before?

Joanna, a companion of the disciples

Then he opened their minds to understand the scriptures, and he said to them, 'Thus it is written, that the Messiah is to suffer and to rise from the dead on the third day, and that repentance and forgiveness of sins is to be proclaimed in his name to all nations, beginning from Jerusalem. You are witnesses of these things.'

Luke 24:45–48

Meditation

How did we not see it before?
How could we have missed what was staring us in the face?
It's a puzzle to me,
to us all,
but that's the way it was.
When they arrested Jesus in the garden,
dragged him before Pilate;
when they nailed him to that cross
and sealed him in a tomb;
we'd believed that was it,
the dream over,
the adventure at an end.
After all, we saw he was dead with our own eyes,
watched him draw his last breath,
so there could be no denying it,
no clutching at straws.
We wanted to, heaven knows!
But what was the point of pretending there was hope,
when it was all too clear there was none.
So we'd simply given in to sorrow,
a paralysing, consuming grief,
and we'd be wrestling with that now, had nothing changed.
But change it did,
wonderfully,

gloriously –
death defeated,
the Lord risen!
He's been with us again today,
laughing, smiling, eating in our presence,
unmistakably alive,
and as he opened the Scriptures to us,
just as he'd done earlier for our friends on the Emmaus Road,
the truth suddenly became obvious,
leaping out at us from the page.
It was as he'd said:
the Messiah must suffer and rise from the dead on the third day –
the empty tomb not the undoing of some awful catastrophe
but part of God's plan,
the fulfilment of his purpose of old.
We hadn't seen it before,
and no doubt there's much we still don't see,
but we know one thing now for sure:
that he's constantly with us,
leading us to a greater understanding of truth
and richer experience of his love,
each day a new beginning through his resurrection life.

Prayer

Loving God,
we have begun to understand the miracle of Easter,
but so much escapes us;
we have grasped a little of your resurrection power,
but have far more still to learn.
We read the Scriptures,
but too often we do not see what's there before us.
We declare our faith,
but our commitment is limited.
Open our eyes,
our minds
and our hearts to the living Christ,
so that we may know the truth more fully
and celebrate each day the new life you have won for us through him.
Amen.

28

I'll never be able to say what it meant to me

Mary Magdalene

Suddenly Jesus met them and said, 'Greetings!' And they came to him, took hold of his feet, and worshipped him. Then Jesus said to them, 'Do not be afraid; go and tell my brothers to go to Galilee; there they will see me.'

Matthew 28:9, 10

Meditation

I'll never be able to say what it meant to me,
after the horror and the heartache,
the darkness and the despair,
to hear that wonderful, astonishing news –
Jesus, alive!
I'd lived in a daze until then,
unable to take in the horror of what I'd seen,
the anguish and the agony that he'd borne
with such quiet dignity and awesome courage.
He'd warned us to expect the worst,
and I suppose in our hearts we'd known what was coming
but we'd refused to accept it,
hoping against hope there might be some other way,
a path less costly, less awful for us all.
But as we walked that morning to the tomb,
all such thoughts were gone,
buried along with our Lord,
life dark, cold, empty,
bereft of meaning.
We were blind to everything in our grief,
scarcely aware even of the ground starting to shake
or light flooding around us,
but when we reached the stone, rolled away from the tomb,

we saw *that* all right,
and for a moment we just stood there gazing in confusion,
not knowing where to turn or what to say.
That's when it came, the news that took our breath away:
'He is not here.
He has been raised.
Come, see the place where he lay.'
We scarcely dared to look at first, afraid it might all be a dream,
but finally we found the courage,
and it was true,
he was gone! –
just the grave clothes left to show he'd been there.
You can imagine how we felt,
our hearts pounding with excitement;
but there was more to come,
things yet more wonderful,
for even as we ran to tell the news,
skipping with sheer delight,
we saw him ahead of us –
Jesus, the man we knew and loved,
arms outstretched in welcome,
waiting to greet us in his old familiar way.
He had risen, just as we'd been told,
death unable to hold him!
Only it wasn't just Jesus who rose that day,
it was all of us:
for there in the garden life began again,
life which we thought had died in us for ever –
hope reborn,
faith renewed,
love rekindled,
joy restored –
and we knew then these could never be destroyed –
the proof was there before us!

Prayer

Gracious God,
through the resurrection of your Son
you not only raised him to life;
you brought also renewal and restoration
to his broken disciples.
From the depths of misery you brought jubilation,
from the pit of despair, hope;
from the trough of doubt, faith.
Life that had seemed without meaning
suddenly pulsated with purpose again,
the future rich with promise as never before.
Thank you for re-enacting that miracle
in countless lives across the centuries
and for continuing to do so today,
reaching out wherever there is need,
wherever people are broken,
wherever hope has died,
bringing afresh your gift of life.
Gracious God, work within us now,
refresh our hearts and revive our spirits,
and make us a new creation,
through Jesus Christ our Lord.
Amen.

29

What were they playing at?

Annas

While they were going, some of the guard went into the city and told the chief priests everything that had happened.

Matthew 28:11

Meditation

What were they playing at?
What could those soldiers possibly have been thinking of?
We'd been afraid of something like this;
some plot to spirit his body away,
pretend he'd risen from the dead;
so we'd taken precautions,
paid for an armed guard to watch the tomb day and night.
There should have been no way anyone could get near him!
Yet what's happened?
He's disappeared, that's what,
snatched away from beneath their very noses.
And now they've come snivelling back here
with their tails between their legs,
expecting us to believe their pathetic excuses.
It wasn't their fault, apparently,
not fair to blame them.
Well, whose fault was it? That's what I'd like to know!
They were the ones appointed to keep watch,
so how do they explain this shambles?
Or do they really imagine we'll swallow the idea
that he's simply vanished?
I know what happened all right;
they fell asleep, didn't they!
Felt they could take it easy,
enjoy a quiet forty winks when our backs were turned,
and no one any the wiser.
The fools!

Can't they see what they've done?
They've gone and played right into his followers' hands;
given them just the opportunity they were looking for.
We'll never hear the last of this now, I can tell you that.
It will be all round the city by tomorrow –
Jesus of Nazareth, the man we had executed for blasphemy,
miraculously come back to life;
one in the eye for the authorities,
a vindication of everything he stood for.
Well, we can't stop that, I'm afraid,
but we must do something to limit the damage,
at least try and keep this thing in bounds;
otherwise there's no knowing where it might lead.
So we'll play it cool –
no panic,
no losing our heads,
just spread the word that his disciples snatched him away
during the night.
Yes, that should do it –
bodysnatchers, grave-robbers!
Nobody will want to be mixed up with business of that sort.
Who knows, we may yet turn this mess around,
even twist it to our own advantage.
It will cost, of course,
those guards won't admit to sleeping for nothing –
it's a disciplinary offence after all –
but whatever it costs it will be worth it,
for I know what Jesus was like,
the hold he had over people,
the love he managed to win,
allegiance he commanded;
and the last thing we can afford
is for him to hold more power having died
than he ever did when he was alive.

Prayer

Living God,
we praise you for the great truth of Easter –
the message that your love will not be defeated.
When human evil had done its worst,

despite every effort to frustrate your purpose,
still your will triumphed!
The stone was rolled away, the tomb was empty,
Christ had risen!
May that truth fire us each day with new hope,
new confidence
and new enthusiasm,
knowing that whatever obstacles we may face
and whatever may fight against us,
there is nothing, finally,
that will be able to stand in the way of your loving grace.
Amen.

30

They don't know when they are beaten, do they?

Caiaphas

While they were going, some of the guard went into the city and told the chief priests everything that had happened.

Matthew 28:11

Meditation

They don't know when they're beaten, do they,
those followers of Jesus?
I really thought we'd put a stop to their nonsense, once and for all.
When we dragged that so-called Christ of theirs before Pilate,
when we saw them hammer the nails into his hands and feet,
when we watched as they sealed the tomb,
I was convinced that, at last, it was over,
the whole unfortunate business at an end.
After all, who wants a dead Messiah?
What use could he be to anyone?
Preposterous, isn't it!
And yet, apparently not,
for I've received news this morning
that the body has vanished,
spirited away during the night.
God knows how it happened,
but it's the last thing we need right now –
you can just imagine the sort of stories
his followers will come up with,
even that he's been raised from the dead, I shouldn't wonder.
Absurd, I know,
but you'd be surprised what some people
are gullible enough to believe,
and if even a few are taken in, who can say how many might follow?
So you'll understand, won't you, if we mould the truth a little?

Nothing patently false, of course;
just a little fine tuning here and there to fit the facts –
we've got it off to a fine art over the years.
Let's face it, it's obvious who's behind this charade.
I've no idea how they did it,
but somehow those wretched followers of his
must have got past the guards –
no doubt sleeping on the job, the good-for-nothing layabouts.
Anyway, that's the line we're taking,
and a few greased palms should ensure a united front,
enough to dispel any rumours.
There are a few points that trouble me though, I must confess:
how they shifted that stone, for one thing,
and why they left behind his grave clothes, for another –
or was that all designed to add to the illusion?
And what I *really* can't understand is this:
why keep his name alive? –
what do they hope to prove? –
for they must know in their hearts that they're beaten,
the game over.
Even supposing some do fall for their trick,
it can't achieve anything,
for as the months pass without sight or sound of him
they're bound to question eventually,
and what a let-down it will all seem then.
You still have your doubts, even now?
Well, let me ask you this,
a question that should settle it for good:
twenty years from now,
a hundred,
a thousand,
who will talk about Jesus then?
Will anyone remember some obscure carpenter from Nazareth?
Need I say more?

Prayer

Sovereign God,
there is much that conspires against your purpose
and frustrates your will,
so much so that we can lose heart

and stop believing in the coming of your kingdom.
The same must have seemed all the more true
for the followers of Jesus in the days following his death,
but they were to learn through the resurrection
that your purpose can never be defeated,
for you are at work in both the good and the bad.
Give us that same sense of conviction
as we respond to your calling today,
and help us, no matter how hopeless a situation may seem,
to persevere in faith
until our course is completed and the race is won,
through Jesus Christ our Lord.
Amen.

31

I just can't understand what happened

One of the guards at the tomb

While they were going, some of the guard went into the city and told the chief priests everything that had happened. After the priests had assembled with the elders, they devised a plan to give a large sum of money to the soldiers, telling them, 'You must say, "His disciples came by night and stole him away while we were asleep." If this comes to the governor's ears, we will satisfy him and keep you out of trouble.' So they took the money and did as they were directed. And this story is still told among the Jews to this day.

Matthew 28:12–15

Meditation

I just can't understand what happened,
how that body could have disappeared like that
from under our very noses.
Oh, I know what some have suggested –
that his disciples stole him away while we were asleep,
that we took bribes to look the other way,
even that we nipped off for a spot of refreshment,
but take it from me, it's nonsense,
for we were there the whole time,
each watching like a hawk,
on the lookout for any suspicious goings-on,
and I can tell you that no one came near the place all night,
not until those women arrived early the next morning,
and discovered the tomb was empty.
You think *they* were shocked?
How about *us*!
We just stood there, gawping in amazement,
unable to believe our eyes.
It couldn't be,
that's what we kept saying,
no way –

but it was,
no doubt about it.
We should have come clean there and then,
told the world what we knew, even though it made no sense,
but it wasn't that easy,
for we knew that our jobs,
even perhaps our lives were on the line –
the penalty for failure.
So when those priests sidled up with their offer of money –
a generous bonus to keep our mouths shut,
and the promise to square things with the governor –
well, understandably we took it;
we'd have been fools not to.
Yet it still rankled,
still stuck in the craw –
not just the dressing-down we received, fierce though that was,
but the stain on our reputation,
the stigma of supposedly having fallen down on the job –
so I'm taking the chance, at last, to put the record straight.
There was no foul-up that night –
we knew our job and stuck to it faithfully.
Don't forget we were Roman soldiers,
proud of our legion,
dedicated to our job –
we'd a reputation to keep up,
and there was no way we were going to let the side down.
No, don't look at us, we weren't to blame.
But if not us, then who?
And, more important, how?
For one thing's certain:
that body was there when they sealed the tomb –
we saw it for ourselves –
but next morning it was gone,
vanished apparently into thin air!
Something happened that night,
something quite extraordinary.
Can you explain it?
I wish I could.

Prayer

Sovereign God,
we don't understand how you raised Jesus from the dead –
how you breathed life into his broken body,
how you rolled the stone away from the tomb,
how he appeared unrecognised to Mary in the garden
and to disciples on the Emmaus road;
how he walked through locked doors to be with the apostles;
how repeatedly he appeared from nowhere
to stand among his followers.
What we do understand is this –
that he changed the lives of all who met him,
turning their sorrow into celebration,
their despair into hope
and their doubt into faith;
and that he is with us now through his life-giving Spirit,
remaking our lives in turn,
giving us joy, peace and a sense of purpose
such as we never imagined possible before.
We do not understand,
but we believe,
we rejoice
and we offer you our grateful worship
in the name of that same Jesus,
our risen Lord and Saviour.
Amen.

32

Three times he asked me

Peter

When they had finished breakfast, Jesus said to Simon Peter, 'Simon son of John, do you love me more than these?' He said to him, 'Yes, Lord; you know that I love you.' Jesus said to him, 'Feed my lambs.' A second time he said to him, 'Simon son of John, do you love me?' He said to him, 'Yes, Lord; you know that I love you.' Jesus said to him, 'Tend my sheep.' He said to him the third time, 'Simon son of John, do you love me?' Peter felt hurt because he said to him the third time, 'Do you love me?' And he said to him, 'Lord, you know everything; you know that I love you.' Jesus said to him, 'Feed my sheep.'

John 21:15–17

Meditation

Three times he asked me,
three times the same simple yet searching question:
'Do you love me, Peter?'
And I was getting fed up with it,
not to say a little hurt.
After all, he should have known by then, surely?
I'd followed him for three years,
and I thought we'd become close –
he gave that impression, anyway.
The 'Rock', he'd called me,
the one on whom he'd build his Church –
an expression of trust, if ever there was one –
so how could he doubt me now,
let alone question my love?
But then, of course, I remembered that bold, brash promise of mine:
'Though all become deserters because of you,
I will never desert you' –
and suddenly I understood.
He'd known I would fail, even as I said it,
not only abandon but deny him,

and he knew too how sick I'd felt,
how wretched and ashamed
when the knowledge of my failure finally sunk home.
But there was no anger from him,
no recriminations,
no rebuke.
His concern was for me, not himself,
his sole desire being to wipe the slate clean
and help me to start again,
and this was my chance to deal with the guilt,
to exorcise the demon once and for all.
Three times I'd denied him,
three times he put the question,
and at last I could put the record straight,
declare to him what I should have declared to others:
'Yes, Lord; you know that I love you.'
We couldn't change the past, we both knew that,
but with his help we could put it behind us and change the future,
and that's what he offered me that day;
a new beginning,
a fresh chapter,
life dawning for me as surely as it had dawned again for him.
I was restored,
cleansed,
forgiven,
the ghost finally laid to rest,
and I owed it all to him,
the man whom I abandoned so swiftly,
yet who refused to abandon me!

Prayer

Gracious God,
we try so hard to put the past behind us,
to let go and start again,
but all too often mistakes we imagined were long buried
return to haunt us.
We do our best to make amends,
but there are times when,
even if *we* can learn to live with the wounds,
others can't,

scars running deep and hurts being hard to forget.
But you are always ready to offer us a new beginning,
no matter how foolish we have been
or how many opportunities we have wasted.
Whatever we may have done,
you grant us free and total forgiveness,
a new page on which to start a fresh chapter.
The past is done with,
the future is before us –
and nothing can ever change that.
Receive our thanks and lead us forward,
in the name of Christ our Saviour.
Amen.

33

Why didn't he call someone like me?

A shepherd

'Very truly, I tell you, anyone who does not enter the sheepfold by the gate but climbs in by another way is a thief and a bandit. The one who enters by the gate is the shepherd of the sheep. The gatekeeper opens the gate for him, and the sheep hear his voice. He calls his own sheep by name and leads them out.'

John 10:1–3

Meditation

Why didn't he call someone like me,
a shepherd, to join his disciples?
It was his choice, of course,
but to my mind he got the balance wrong:
too many fishermen by half!
Oh, I've nothing against them;
it's just that as well as fishing for people
aren't we also to care for sheep,
to look after those we've got
as well as trawl for more?
After all, *we* were the first to see Jesus,
the first after his parents to welcome him into the world.
So why shut us out afterwards,
as though we don't count?
Only that's not quite true, is it?
No one's excluded:
not us,
not anyone.
But what Jesus needed at the start was fishers of men,
people to go out in his name and proclaim the good news,
spreading the word far and wide.
Would *we* have done that?
Would we have looked inwards or outwards?
I'm not sure,

but I'm certain of this:
if others had failed to spread their net on his behalf
I wouldn't be here now –
wouldn't have heard the message
and made my response.
No, we need both fisherman and shepherds,
evangelists and pastors,
but though both are important
one's vital.
Maybe he made the right choice after all.

Prayer

God of all,
help us to share our faith sincerely and effectively –
through word and deed to make known what you mean to us,
what you have done in our lives,
what you have accomplished in Christ.
Though we may not be gifted with words,
still less accomplished as evangelists,
may who and what we are speak unmistakably of you,
testifying to your transforming grace and life-giving power.
Imbue us with peace,
joy,
gentleness,
compassion,
wisdom,
generosity,
and, above all, love,
so that our lives may meaningfully proclaim your name
and reflect your glory.
Amen.

34

To what lengths would I go in looking after my sheep?

A shepherd

'I am the good shepherd. The good shepherd lays down his life for the sheep. The hired hand, who is not the shepherd and does not own the sheep, sees the wolf coming and leaves the sheep and runs away – and the wolf snatches them and scatters them. The hired hand runs away because a hired hand does not care for the sheep. I am the good shepherd. I know my own and my own know me, just as the Father knows me and I know the Father. And I lay down my life for the sheep.'

John 10:11–15

Meditation

To what lengths would I go in looking after my sheep?
That's a good question.
I'd watch over them night and day if I had to,
for it's dangerous country out there,
and there are wild animals aplenty that would make a meal of them
given half a chance.
I'd search for them too, should they be lost,
and yes, defend them if necessary, provided I was suitably armed.
But knowingly surrender my life for them?
No, I'd draw the line at that.
After all, it's sheep we're talking about, nothing more,
a way of earning a living –
keeping a roof over one's head
and money in one's pocket.
There's no room for sentimental attachment.
Would any go further?
Certainly none I know of.
A hired hand wouldn't, that's for sure;
they'd run a mile at the first whiff of danger;
and even the most dedicated among us would save their own skin first
if push came to shove.

No, I've heard of some fine shepherds in my time,
but to lay down your life for your sheep would be something else.
Could any flock be worth it?

Prayer

Lord Jesus Christ,
words cannot thank you enough for your goodness to us –
for your patience, concern and devotion.
Repeatedly we go astray,
yet you seek us out,
never resting until we are found.
We ignore your guidance,
yet you continue to call,
gently leading us back.
Though we are foolish and fickle,
naively following the crowd,
you stay true to us,
refusing to let us go.
For your awesome love that gave everything to bring us life,
receive our grateful praise and heartfelt worship.
Amen.

35

Why didn't he tell us who he was?

A Sadducee listening to Jesus

So the Jews gathered around him and said to him, 'How long will you keep us in suspense? If you are the Messiah, tell us plainly.' Jesus answered, 'I have told you, and you do not believe. The works that I do in my Father's name testify to me; but you do not believe, because you do not belong to my sheep. My sheep hear my voice. I know them, and they follow me. I give them eternal life, and they will never perish. No one will snatch them out of my hand.'

John 10:24–28

Meditation

Why didn't he tell us who he was?
Why beat about the bush,
talking in parables and riddles,
when he could have made things clear?
Was he the Messiah or wasn't he?
But he wouldn't come clean,
seeming determined instead to keep us guessing.
Well, what could we make of that?
It seemed obvious he wasn't the Messiah,
but that he wanted us to think he might be;
that, despite all his claims to the contrary,
he enjoyed the mystique,
the attentions of the crowd,
and wanted to keep it going.
Even then, though, we wanted to believe,
hoping we might be wrong,
so we put him on the spot,
asking him to give it to us straight,
one way or the other.
And what did he talk about in reply?
Sheep!
I know: extraordinary, isn't it!

He seemed to imply we had only to listen
and the truth would be revealed,
but that we'd made up our minds already
and were resolved *not* to hear.
What nonsense!
The truth is that, for all his signs and wonders,
God's reign on earth seemed as far away as ever,
consigned to some future kingdom
rather than established here today.
Well, I'm sorry, but we don't go in for all that pie-in-the-sky nonsense,
resurrection and eternal life;
never will, either,
unless someone comes back from the dead to prove it.
Let Jesus do that and we'll revise our opinion,
of him and everything,
for *of course* we'd believe then –
who wouldn't?
But I don't think that's likely.
Do *you*?

Prayer

Living Lord,
in a sceptical and cynical world that refuses to believe,
help us to keep faith in you.
Though we cannot prove you rose again,
or that *we* will either,
may your voice continue to ring true within us,
speaking of your risen presence and promise of life –
a sure and certain hope.
Amen.

36

We were confused when he first told us

Thomas

When he had gone out, Jesus said, 'Now the Son of Man has been glorified, and God has been glorified in him. If God has been glorified in him, God will also glorify him in himself and will glorify him at once. Little children, I am with you only a little longer. You will look for me; and as I said to the Jews so now I say to you, "Where I am going, you cannot come."'

John 13:31–33

Meditation

We were confused when he first told us,
not to mention disappointed,
for we'd assumed somehow that he'd be with us always,
constantly there by our sides.
What was all this about leaving,
going where none of us could follow?
We didn't like such talk at all.
But if we were puzzled then,
it was as nothing compared to what came later,
after he rose again,
for just as we were celebrating his return,
beside ourselves with excitement,
he came up with the same idea,
telling us he had to leave us once more.
'*Why?*' we wondered.
Couldn't he stay,
if not for ever then at least for a time?
What was so pressing,
so important,
that he had to disappear once more,
and this time, apparently, for good?
We wanted to keep him with us,
to go back to how things had been before:
us and him together.

And so, as it turned out, we *have*,
though not quite in the way we thought,
for he's with us still through his Spirit,
not just by our side but within.
Only by leaving could he truly draw close.
Only through departing this earth
could he open the gates of heaven
that we might one day follow where he's gone
There could be no standing still or remaining the same,
for his place was with the Father
as King of kings and Lord of lords,
enthroned in glory on high.
We've learnt, finally, what that means:
that he's bigger than *us*,
bigger than Judea,
bigger than we'd ever imagined,
his dying and rising,
mercy and love,
not just for a few
but for all.

Prayer

Forgive us, Lord,
for we tie you down to our narrow horizons,
our limited parochial concerns,
forgetting that you are exalted over all,
enthroned on high,
your purpose reaching to the ends of the earth
in every place and time.
Enlarge our vision,
broaden our understanding,
so that, in glimpsing your greatness,
we may recognise also the extent of your love –
the height, depth, length and breadth of who and what you are,
and what that means,
for us
and for all.
Amen.

37

'Show us the Father,' I asked

Philip

'In my Father's house there are many dwelling places. If it were not so, would I have told you that I go to prepare a place for you? And if I go and prepare a place for you, I will come again and will take you to myself, so that where I am, there you may be also. And you know the way to the place where I am going.' Thomas said to him, 'Lord, we do not know where you are going. How can we know the way?' Jesus said to him, 'I am the way, and the truth, and the life. No one comes to the Father except through me. If you know me, you will know my Father also. From now on you do know him and have seen him.' Philip said to him, 'Lord, show us the Father, and we will be satisfied.'

John 14:2–8

Meditation

'Show us the Father,' I asked.
Can you believe that!
After three years of following Jesus,
three years of walking by his side,
still I could come up with a daft line like that!
It makes me cringe now to think of it,
but at the time,
despite all he'd said,
it seemed perfectly sensible,
the most natural request in the world.
I was coming at things the wrong way, you see,
wanting all my questions answered –
as though I could understand everything about God,
all there is to know,
down to the very last detail.
And I'd no need –
that's the stupid thing –
for I'd seen him already,
there by my side in Jesus.

In his words,
his deeds,
his love,
his mercy,
God was present –
like Father, like Son,
the Word made flesh –
but I couldn't see for looking,
the wood obscured by the trees.
Learn from my mistake,
or you may search eagerly for God
yet never find.
We'll never understand *everything*,
not in this life,
not until we see him face to face,
but in Jesus we've seen enough and more than enough:
all we need to know.

Prayer

Almighty God,
thank you that, for all your splendour,
all your majesty, power and glory,
we can not only know *about* you
but know you *personally*,
your greatness having been revealed in Christ,
your purpose fulfilled through him.
Thank you for, through him, bringing the divine down to earth,
making it real for us in such a way that we can see and understand it,
relating who and what you are to our daily lives.
Help us, if we would know you better,
to focus our thoughts on Jesus,
one with us yet one also with you.
Amen.

38

He'd talked of his Father's house

Philip

Jesus answered him, 'Those who love me will keep my word, and my Father will love them, and we will come to them and make our home with them. I have said these things to you while I am still with you. But the Advocate, the Holy Spirit, whom the Father will send in my name, will teach you everything, and remind you of all that I have said to you.'

John 14:23, 25, 26

Meditation

He'd talked of his Father's house,
of going there to prepare a place for us,
and that had seemed wonderful enough.
But then he went further,
and his words, if anything, were more wonderful,
more incredible still,
for he spoke of coming –
with the Father,
through his Spirit –
and making his home among us.
Imagine that:
God living *within*,
Jesus alive in our hearts,
divine love and power coursing through our veins!
It would change everything,
our thoughts, words and deeds,
making faith real in a way it's never been before.
Can it be possible,
sharing our life with the Lord of all,
walking and talking with the creator God –
mighty and majestic,
yet one with you and I?
It seemed too good to be true,
especially after they nailed him to a cross and sealed him in a tomb,

but it wasn't,
for he came back, just as he'd promised,
triumphant over the grave,
and now I know beyond doubt he'll come again,
not just in the fullness of time
but in the here and now,
God indeed dwelling among us
if only we'll welcome him in.

Prayer

Lord Jesus Christ,
make your dwelling place within us.
Fill us with your Spirit
in heart, mind and soul
so that your living presence shapes who and what were are.
Come afresh into our lives,
and direct everything we think and say and do,
so that we shall live more fully as your people,
bringing glory to you.
Amen.

39

He knew what he was talking about, Jesus

A vineyard owner

'I am the true vine, and my Father is the vine-grower. He removes every branch in me that bears no fruit. Every branch that bears fruit he prunes to make it bear more fruit.'

John 15:1, 2

Meditation

He knew what was he was talking about, Jesus.
Growing grapes is no easy business,
certainly not something you can leave to take care of itself.
The vine has to be pruned carefully,
dead wood cut out,
healthy growth encouraged,
and then there's the training of stems to see to,
the protecting from pests,
the feeding, watering and weeding,
before harvest can finally come.
It's about the vine and the grower,
the two working together,
and that's what we need to remember in terms of the *true* vine,
and growing in him.
Too easily we make it about *us*,
our efforts,
our attempts to bear fruit –
believe me, *I* know,
for I've done it all too often myself.
But that's like saying a grape can grow on its own,
or that *we're* the vine ourselves –
the whole perspective hopelessly skewed.
It's God who gives growth,
not us,

and it comes through being in Christ,
not through anything *we* might do.
You can't produce a crop alone, however hard you try;
at least, not fruit of the Spirit.
Remain close to him,
nourished and nurtured by his love,
for then, and only then, will your life yield the harvest he seeks.

Prayer

Loving God,
we like to think we are productive in your service,
that our discipleship is truly fruitful,
but in our more honest moments we know that is rarely the case,
so much in our lives instead being dead wood.
We promise plenty but deliver little,
whether through disobedience or negligence –
through rejecting your will
or through failing to make time for you
so that you can nourish and nurture our faith.
We forget that real growth comes not through our own efforts,
however sincere,
but by your grace.
Forgive the barrenness of our commitment,
and help us to be truly one with you,
so that we may grow in faith
and bear lasting fruit of your Spirit.
Amen.

40

Oh no, not another rule to follow!

Philip and Thomas

'As the Father has loved me, so I have loved you; abide in my love. If you keep my commandments, you will abide in my love, just as I have kept my Father's commandments and abide in his love. I have said these things to you so that my joy may be in you, and that your joy may be complete. This is my commandment, that you love one another as I have loved you.'

John 15:9–12

Meditation

Philip Oh no, not another rule to follow! –
that's what we thought at first.
After all, that's what we were used to,
what we'd grown up with for as long as we could remember.

Thomas Faith was about doing this, doing that –
not just *ten* commandments,
but a host of others,
decrees for just about every eventuality under the sun.

Philip We're not knocking it,
for it helped to fashion our nation,
and by and large, with the odd aberration,
it's kept us on the straight and narrow.

Thomas But we don't mind admitting that, like many others,
we've found it a struggle,
both to observe the requirements of the Law
and to feel it's got us anywhere,
put us right with God.

Philip Was Jesus going to give us a new system, we wondered,
a different set of rules?

Thomas No, he summed up his way instead in a single sentence,
devastatingly simple,
yet infinitely challenging:

Philip 'This is my commandment:
that you love one another
as I have loved you.'
Thomas Wow, we thought –
that sounds easy!
Philip But, of course, it's not;
in his case it meant death on a cross,
total self-surrender –
that's how costly love can be.
Thomas We'll never show anything quite like that,
but it's the yardstick we measure ourselves by,
the goal we aim for,
shaping everything we think, and say, and do.
Philip It's what the Law, gospel and God himself is all about,
the heart of our faith:
love!
Thomas Not just a new commandment,
but the greatest commandment of all.

Prayer

Gracious God,
the good news is so simple and straightforward,
but we make it so complicated,
burying the message of the gospel under a mountain of dogma.
You call us to love you and one another,
just as you love us,
but instead we turn discipleship into jumping through doctrinal hoops,
assenting to theological niceties.
We allow ourselves to be taken in by claims that love is vague,
wishy-washy;
that we need moral absolutes spelt out for each and every situation;
whereas, in fact, love is the most demanding option of all.
Give us the courage, strength and faith we need
to walk the way of Christ.
Amen.

41

There were things he felt unable to tell us at the time

Peter, James and John

'I still have many things to say to you, but you cannot bear them now. When the Spirit of truth comes, he will guide you into all the truth; for he will not speak on his own, but will speak whatever he hears, and he will declare to you the things that are to come. He will glorify me, because he will take what is mine and declare it to you.'

John 16:12–14

Meditation

Peter There were things he felt unable to tell us at the time,
not because he didn't want to or had something to hide,
but because we simply weren't ready to hear them.
John We weren't expecting his death, for a start,
each of us still secretly hoping he'd reign on earth, here and now.
James And if we weren't prepared for his death,
we weren't ready either for his resurrection.
None of us believed the tomb was empty,
not at first.
We thought it was nonsense, do you recall?
John It was his return to the Father, though, that got me most –
I just couldn't get my head round it.
One moment he was back by our side,
and the next gone again,
or so it seemed at the time.
Peter And as for the gift of Spirit,
power from on high,
well, he may have promised it often enough,
but we'd no idea what he actually meant.
It took us by surprise completely!

John Yes, we've come a long way
since we rode with him into Jerusalem,
the crowds welcoming him as king.
He'd told us what to expect,
but we couldn't even take *that* in at first,
let alone more.

James And he continues to astonish us, even now,
the Spirit time and again offering fresh insights
into the things he taught us.

Peter We needed time to learn,
to accept,
to grow,
and, of course, we still do,
for we're talking here of the things of God,
of grasping the unseen.

James It needs patience to do that,

John trust,

Peter discipline,

James a life lived with him.

John We're on a journey of faith,

James and we've not finished it yet,

Peter not by a long way.

All We've only just begun.

Prayer

Mighty and mysterious God,
we like to think we know it all –
that we have understood the gospel
and grasped the wonder of who and what you are.
But the reality is different,
for your ways are not our ways
or your thoughts our thoughts.
So much is beyond us,
leaving us baffled and bemused,
and much else is at best only partially fathomed.
Time and again what we thought we knew is challenged and tested,
needing to be either revised or discarded altogether.
Give us the humility we need
to accept that our knowledge is incomplete,

that there is always more to learn.
Open our hearts to the great adventure of discovery you set before us,
until that day when we finally see you face to face,
and know you, even as we are fully known.
Amen.

42

I couldn't help overhearing his words

The Apostle James

After Jesus had spoken these words, he looked up to heaven and said, 'Father, the hour has come; glorify your Son so that the Son may glorify you . . . I have made your name known to those whom you gave me from the world. They were yours, and you gave them to me, and they have kept your word . . . And now I am no longer in the world, but they are in the world, and I am coming to you. Holy Father, protect them in your name that you have given me, so that they may be one, as we are one.'

John 17:1, 6, 11

Meditation

I couldn't help overhearing his words,
that night in the garden before our world fell apart
and they nailed him to a cross.
He was praying,
pouring out his soul to God,
and as I listened my spirit soared,
for it seemed as though our hopes were about to realised
and our fears prove unfounded –
that instead of sorrow and death there would be a happy ending,
our Lord recognised by all,
acclaimed and worshipped,
enthroned in glory.
He spoke of authority from God,
of fulfilling the mission he'd been sent to achieve,
so I put two and two together and made five,
assuming he expected the dawn of God's kingdom here on earth
and deliverance at last for his people.
I was right in a way, of course,
for he achieved precisely that,
but he did so through a cross rather than crown,
through apparent defeat rather than trumpeted victory,
and at first we just couldn't see it.

I'd assumed he was praying for himself back there in Gethsemane –
that he'd begged God to provide another way,
less costly,
undemanding,
and that God might somehow oblige –
but I'd misread things completely,
for his entreaties were for *our* welfare rather than his own,
for all who would come after him,
for the world itself.
That's what mattered most, even at such a time,
not *his* fate but *ours* –
that we should share his joy, his life, his kingdom,
now and for all eternity.

Prayer

Lord Jesus Christ,
we marvel at the extent of your love,
at the fact that,
in life and in death,
your thoughts were all for *us*
and none for *you*.
We rejoice in your gift of life –
abundant,
eternal,
overflowing –
won for us by your selfless devotion to our cause;
your willingness to suffer in body, mind and spirit,
surrendering all.
Though we will never get anywhere near such commitment,
help us, in turn,
to put the welfare of others before our own,
denying ourselves for their sake and for yours.
Amen.

43

What did he come to give us?

The apostles

'Now they know that everything you have given me is from you; for the words that you gave to me I have given to them, and they have received them and know in truth that I came from you; and they have believed that you sent me. But now I am coming to you, and I speak these things in the world so that they may have my joy made complete in themselves.'

John 17:7, 8, 13

Meditation

1 What did he come to give us?
2 *Light*, say some,
and they're right enough,
for he's shone in the darkness of this world,
bringing good out of evil,
right out of wrong –
a new dawn for all.
3 *Grace*, say others,
and they have a point,
for undeserving though we are,
unworthy of his blessing,
he pours out his mercy, time and again.
4 I'd go for *truth*,
for he's shown us the way,
the answer to our deepest needs –
God's word made flesh,
setting us free.
5 *Peace* would be my choice,
an inner tranquillity of spirit,
unlike anything this world can give,
passing understanding.
6 I'd opt for *life*,
resurrection life,
lived not just now, in all its fullness,
but with him for evermore.

7 Ah, but what about love?
Isn't that the key to it all –
the meaning of the Law and prophets,
heart of the gospel,
and essence of God?
8 No question of that,
no question of any,
but one thing joins them all.
'I speak these things in the world,' he said,
'so that they may have my joy made complete in themselves.'
That's what he gives,
that's what sums up everything he's done:
an inner happiness that no one can take away –
his joy complete in our hearts.

Prayer

Living God,
we have so much to celebrate,
so many reasons to give thanks,
for you have richly blessed us,
showering us with good things.
Yet do our lives radiate the joy of Christ?
We speak of it,
sing of it,
but would anyone around us take note of a happiness that sets us apart?
Help us truly to appreciate all you have done and given,
so that the joy we proclaim may unmistakably shine from us.
Teach us to exult in your unfailing love and mercy,
and to rejoice in each day you have made,
through Jesus Christ our Lord.
Amen.

44

We couldn't go where he was going

Andrew

'Father, I desire that those also, whom you have given me, may be with me where I am, to see my glory, which you have given me because you loved me before the foundation of the world.'

John 17:24–26

Meditation

We couldn't go where he was going,
he'd told us that before,
and though we didn't understand it at the time,
we did later,
for he was taken into heaven
to share in the Father's glory.
To be honest, we didn't *want* to go with him,
not if it meant leaving this world so soon for the next.
We'd a life to live
and a job to do:
the message of his love and purpose needing to be shared with others,
proclaimed throughout the world.
And after he rose again and was taken from us,
exalted by the Father,
we resolved to do just that:
to proclaim his love and work for his kingdom,
on earth as it is in heaven.
Yet, of course, this world,
for all its blessings,
is not an end in itself
but a taste of things to come,
and though we can't be with him now,
he's promised that one day we shall be,
each privileged to enter his kingdom
and witness his glory.
I can't say more –

no one can –
for though we've glimpsed a little,
our knowledge is incomplete,
but from what we've experienced already,
the love, joy and peace he's so richly given,
we know that his word is true,
his promise certain:
the best is yet to come.

Prayer

Thank you, Lord, for the wonder of life
and the beauty of this world –
so much around us that moves us to delight and wonder,
filling our hearts with praise.
Thank you for your presence with us in the here and now,
the way you so faithfully bless us
and give meaning to our lives.
But thank you, above all, for what you hold in store,
the joy that awaits us in your kingdom,
greater than anything our hearts can yet conceive,
special beyond words.
Amen.

45

He spoke with conviction, that man

Dionysius the Areopagite

Then Paul said, 'While God has overlooked the times of human ignorance, now he commands all people everywhere to repent, because he has fixed a day on which he will have the world judged in righteousness by a man whom he has appointed, and of this he has given assurance to all by raising him from the dead.' When they heard of the resurrection of the dead, some scoffed; but others said, 'We will hear you again about this.' At that point Paul left them. But some of them joined him and became believers, including Dionysius the Areopagite and a woman named Damaris, and others with them.

Acts 17:22a, 30, 34

Meditation

He spoke with conviction, that man,
I'll give him that –
as though he totally believed what he was saying.
The arguments may have been weak sometimes,
not the same sophistication, subtlety, as our own philosophers;
and as an orator, to put it bluntly, I've heard better.
But he tried,
he really tried to get his message home,
more than anyone else I've ever met.
He'd done his homework too, that was clear,
speaking to us in terms we would understand,
language we could immediately relate to.
And he wasn't just playing games,
out to prove some academic point or make his mark as a speaker.
You could see he was sincere,
desperate to get his message home.
One rarely hears that here, you know,
here where ideas are two a penny
and schools of thought vie together like brawling children,
each resolved to win the day.

I've sat and listened many times
while good and evil,
life and death
are toyed with in debate like a toddler's plaything –
diverting,
rewarding for a time,
but then casually put aside until another day.
Not Paul though –
he talked as one who *had* to speak,
of things that burned within him,
his eyes aflame and face aglow.
I won't say I'm convinced,
not yet at least;
I'll have to hear him further before I go that far.
But I'm intrigued,
eager to find out more,
for when he spoke of death and then of life,
of Jesus rising from the tomb,
he talked as one who knew,
who'd seen,
who had no doubts.
Well, if he's right and Jesus really is alive,
if he spoke truth and this man really rose,
then I want to meet him, see him for myself;
not put my trust in another's faith
but root it in my own.
Can it be true?
It seems impossible,
too good for words.
Yet there's no denying it, despite what his critics may say –
he spoke with conviction, that man,
with a passion I have rarely heard,
and a passion I would love to share.

Prayer

Loving God,
you do not call us all to be evangelists or preachers of your word,
but you do call us all to be witnesses,
telling others what Jesus has done for us.
And through Paul you have shown us what really counts
if we are to do that effectively,
not using clever words
or presenting carefully rehearsed arguments,
but simply speaking openly and honestly from the heart.
Loving God,
as we have heard,
so may we tell.
Amen.

46

'What will it be like?' they ask me

The Apostle Paul

But someone will ask, 'How are the dead raised? With what kind of body do they come?' Fool! What you sow does not come to life unless it dies . . . So it is with the resurrection of the dead. What is sown is perishable, what is raised is imperishable. It is sown in dishonour, it is raised in glory. It is sown in weakness, it is raised in power. It is sown a physical body, it is raised a spiritual body.

1 Corinthians 15:35, 36; 42–44a

Meditation

'What will it be like?' they ask me.
'What sort of body will we have?
What sort of clothes?
What sort of food?'
And then, as if that weren't enough,
'When will it be?
Where will we go?
How will it happen?'
As if *I* should know!
All right, so maybe I did catch a glimpse of life outside the body,
but that doesn't make me an expert, does it –
an authority on the life to come?
Yet admit that to some people
and they start to question everything,
as though the whole idea of resurrection
hinges on our ability to understand it.
I know why they ask, of course I do,
for it's not easy living with mystery,
accepting claims one cannot fathom or even begin to picture;
yet is that really anything new
when it comes to the things of God?
'My thoughts are not your thoughts,
nor your ways my ways' –

isn't that what he told us,
so why presume they are?
I realised long ago that,
just because we don't understand something,
doesn't mean it isn't true.
The trouble is we start in the wrong place,
looking to what's yet to be rather than what's been already,
but it's there that our faith rests:
in the wonder of the empty tomb,
the folded grave clothes,
the risen Lord;
in the glorious message of his victory over death,
his final triumph over evil.
Isn't that enough for you?
It is for me.
I can't explain how it happened, but I know it's real,
for I've met him myself,
experienced his presence,
died, through his power, to the old self and risen to the new.
Take away that, and you take away everything.
We'd all like to know more, I accept that,
to end, once and for all, the guessing and speculation,
but we wouldn't understand even if it was spelt out for us,
for the things God has in store
are beyond the human eye to see or heart to conceive.
So no more brooding about the future –
what *may* be,
what *could* be.
Think rather of Christ –
what he's *done*,
what he's *doing*,
and then you will learn to take on trust
the things he's yet to do,
and the life that yet *shall* be.

Prayer

Sovereign God,
you do not ask us to base our faith on what might be
but on what *has* been and what *is*.
You came to our world in Christ and lived among us,

demonstrating your commitment to humankind.
Through him you suffered and died on a cross,
but in triumph you rose again,
testifying to your victory over death.
And now, through that same Jesus,
we experience the daily reality of your presence
and the constant wonder of your love.
May all you have done and continue to do
inspire us to trust in the future you hold for us,
confident that as you are with us now
so you will be for all eternity,
through Jesus Christ our Lord.
Amen.

47

One day we'll see him again

John the Evangelist

Then I saw a new heaven and a new earth; for the first heaven and the first earth had passed away, and the sea was no more. And I saw the holy city, the new Jerusalem, coming down out of heaven from God, prepared as a bride adorned for her husband. And I heard a loud voice from the throne saying, 'See, the home of God is among mortals. He will dwell with them as their God; they will be his peoples, and God himself will be with them; he will wipe every tear from their eyes. Death will be no more; mourning and crying and pain will be no more, for the first things have passed away.'

Revelation 21:1–4

Meditation

One day we'll see him again.
Don't ask me when or how,
but one day
when all this struggle is over –
the pain,
the grief,
the fear,
the doubt –
then he will return to establish his kingdom.
I know that's hard to believe sometimes.
When you keep on battling against the odds
and nothing seems to change,
when you stand up for what is good yet evil seems to triumph –
love met with hatred,
gentleness with violence,
and truth with falsehood –
of course you start to wonder.
When you're faced with suffering, sickness, death;
when greed and corruption are rewarded with plenty
and justice is trampled underfoot;

when the poor get poorer and the world goes by uncaring –
it's impossible not to ask yourself, day after day,
why it's allowed to happen.
But he will come, I'm certain of it –
not just because he promised to,
though that's important, of course;
nor simply because he came back before,
cheating death of its victory,
triumphing over the grave,
though that's more vital still;
but because he *has* to return if anything is finally to make sense,
if faith is to be more than a grand delusion.
And it *is* more;
it *has* to be.
These goals we strive towards,
this life revealed in Christ,
the promises he made,
truths he taught,
everything he lived and died for –
they've turned my life around,
sustained me through my darkest moments,
and given me a joy that knows no bounds.
So though we do not understand and faith is hard,
we'll hold fast to hope,
waiting for that time when sorrow and suffering will be no more;
a time when he will live among his people
and we shall see him again,
crowned in glory and splendour,
King of kings,
Lord of lords,
all in all,
yet one with us!

Prayer

Living God,
through Christ you have taught us to pray,
'Thy kingdom come, thy will be done.'
We look forward to the day when that prayer is answered:
a day when there will be no more night,
no more darkness,
an end to mourning and crying and pain –
to death itself.
Sustain us, we pray, through all the uncertainties of our fleeting lives
with that sure and certain hope.
Amen!

48

I had a dream last night

John the Evangelist

Nothing accursed will be found there any more. But the throne of God and of the Lamb will be in it, and his servants will worship him; they will see his face, and his name will be on their foreheads. And there will be no more night; they need no light of lamp or sun, for the Lord God will be their light, and they will reign for ever and ever.

Revelation 22:3–5

Meditation

I had a dream last night,
a wonderful, astonishing dream –
so vivid that it will live with me for the rest of my days.
I caught a glimpse of God,
enthroned in majesty,
encircled by the great company of heaven,
and there at his right hand,
exalted,
lifted up in splendour,
was our Lord Jesus Christ.
It was wonderful,
breathtaking,
indescribable.
Yet I have to share it with you somehow –
clutching at metaphors,
searching for the right words,
but at least giving you some idea of what I saw.
'Why?' I hear you say.
What does it matter if it was only a dream?'
And I take your point.
Yet I have this feeling, deep within,
no – more than just a feeling – this certainty,
that God was speaking to me through it:
speaking to *me*,

to *you*,
to everyone with ears to hear and a mind to listen.
He was telling us that in all the chaos of this humdrum world,
all the evil that conspires against him,
God is there,
slowly but surely working out his purpose.
And one day,
in the fullness of time,
his kingdom shall come and his will be done.
Don't ask me when, for I can't tell you that.
But though we may not see or feel it,
I am assured that he will triumph.
Joy will take the place of sorrow.
Life will follow death.
Love will be victorious!

Prayer

Eternal and sovereign God,
you have promised that, one day,
there will be an end to everything that frustrates your will
and denies your love.
You promise us a kingdom in which there will be no more hatred,
no more sorrow and suffering;
a kingdom of everlasting peace filled with light and love and joy.
You promise that death itself shall be overcome
and we shall be raised to life eternal,
one with all your people from every place and time,
and one with you.
That great picture seems like a dream sometimes,
and yet we believe that what you have promised will be done.
May that vision burn bright in our hearts –
a constant source of comfort and inspiration
as we journey in faith towards that final goal.
Walk with us and see us safely through.
Amen.

Ascension Day

49

We had just come, just as he'd told us to

Matthew

Now the eleven disciples went to Galilee, to the mountain to which Jesus had directed them. When they saw him, they worshipped him; but some doubted. And Jesus came and said to them, 'All authority in heaven and on earth has been given to me. Go therefore and make disciples of all nations, baptising them in the name of the Father and of the Son and of the Holy Spirit, and teaching them to obey everything that I have commanded you. And remember, I am with you always, to the end of the age.'

Matthew 28:16–20

Meditation

We had come, just as he'd told us to –
up on to the mountains of Galilee where we'd walked so often,
where we'd sat at the Master's feet,
where we'd watched as he taught the crowds
and marvelled as he fed the multitude –
and suddenly it was just like old times,
for he was there once more,
standing by our side,
that old familiar smile,
that warm, comforting presence,
Jesus, alive and well.
Can you imagine what it felt like,
after the shock, the horror, the disbelief at his death?
We'd been crushed,
distraught,
everything we'd lived and worked for turned to ashes,
and there had seemed no point to anything,
no future,
no hope,
nothing to lift the pall of misery that overwhelmed us.
Do you wonder we fell down and worshipped him!
It was as though we had awoken from some dreadful dream

to find the sun burning bright,
and we were terrified of closing our eyes even for a moment
in case darkness should return and the nightmare begin again.
I know it was foolish, but we actually hoped nothing had changed,
that we could pick up where we'd left off,
and follow once more in the Master's footsteps.
But, of course, we couldn't,
for it *had* changed –
not just him,
but us,
and everything.
They'd laid him in a tomb,
and he'd emerged victorious.
They'd tried to destroy him,
but he could not be defeated.
And it was a message the whole world needed to hear –
the victory of love,
his triumph over evil,
good news not just for us but for all.
Yes, the work *would* continue, just as we'd hoped,
only it needed *us* to carry it forward,
our willingness to speak,
our faith to respond,
our courage to go out and make disciples of all nations,
so that they too might know the risen Christ
and respond in turn.
It could no longer simply be us and him,
much though we might have wished it –
there was work to be done,
a message to share,
a kingdom to build,
and he needed our help to build it.
We'd come and met him, just as he had told us to –
now it was time to go!

Prayer

God of all,
we talk much about witness, evangelism, mission;
about sharing the good news,
being a light to the nations;

but, when it comes to it, our words are rarely backed up by actions.
We focus instead on worship, prayer, private devotion;
on personal growth and times of fellowship;
our minds turned in on the Church
rather than out to the world.
Forgive our lack of faith,
of courage
and of vision,
and give us the words to say,
the will to speak them,
and, above all,
a life that, in every part,
proclaims your glory and tells of your love.
Amen.

50

You'd think we'd have been dismayed, wouldn't you?

Philip

Then he led them out as far as Bethany, and, lifting up his hands, he blessed them. While he was blessing them, he withdrew from them and was carried up into heaven.

Luke 24:50, 51

Meditation

You'd think we'd have been dismayed, wouldn't you –
to lose Jesus again, so soon after he'd come back to us?
After all, we'd been shattered the first time,
left floundering like fish out of water once deprived of his presence.
True, this time was different –
no cross,
no agony, torment and death –
but he was gone nonetheless,
snatched away from us once more.
Only he *wasn't*,
that's the strange thing.
He was with us much more meaningfully,
not in the flesh but in Spirit –
around us,
beside us,
beyond us,
within us,
touching our lives in every part.
I can't quite explain it,
but suddenly we knew he was closer than we'd ever dreamt –
for he was not just the Messiah,
the risen Lord,
but God himself,
one with him,

one with us,
the divine in human form.
We'd walked and talked with him,
and we finally realised that we'd do so always, to the end of time.
No wonder he blessed us when he took his leave,
for though he's far away now at the Father's side,
through his Spirit he couldn't be more near.

Prayer

Creator God,
mighty and mysterious,
awesome beyond words,
thank you for making yourself known to us in Christ –
for sharing our humanity,
walking our earth,
becoming one with us through him.
Lord Jesus Christ,
thank you for breaking down the barriers
that separate us from the Father,
for helping us not just to know but to relate to God firsthand.
Thank you that through your living, dying and rising among us
we can experience the gift of your Spirit,
your living presence deep within.
Open our eyes each day to the wonder of who you are
and of everything you have done,
and help us joyfully to worship you,
our risen, ascended Lord.
Amen.

51

Do you know what we did that day?

Peter

And they worshipped him, and returned to Jerusalem with great joy; and they were continually in the temple blessing God.

Luke 24:52, 53

Meditation

Do you know what we did that day?
We *worshipped* him, that's what:
not God,
but Jesus,
acclaiming him as King of kings and Lord of lords.
Nothing strange in that, you might say,
but there *was*,
although, funnily enough, none of us saw it at the time.
We knelt in homage,
overcome with awe and wonder –
to bow before him seeming as natural as breathing,
the only response that would do.
Yet we're talking of *Jesus*, remember –
the man born in a stable,
killed on a cross,
sealed in a tomb –
flesh and blood like you and me,
as human as any.
We'd followed him,
loved him,
served him . . .
but as one of *us*,
a man with whom we could share our hopes and fears,
joys and sorrows,
knowing he would understand,
having been there too.
Suddenly it was different,
the human divine,

divine human –
but it wasn't God who had altered,
or Jesus . . .
it was *us*,
our perceptions changed for ever.
They were both bigger than we thought –
God nearer,
Jesus greater –
too wonderful for words.
No wonder we worshipped,
no wonder we worship still,
for God had become one with us
that we might be one with him.

Prayer

Lord Jesus Christ,
forgive us,
for too often we fail to glimpse your glory
in the ordinary things of life.
We look for your presence in eye-catching signs and wonders –
some heavenly proof of your power –
when all the time your love, purpose and grace is evident around us
if only our hearts are open to recognise and receive.
Teach us to discern your hand in the events of daily life,
and to grasp that you are both near and far,
here and everywhere,
close by our side yet enthroned in heaven –
truly the King of kings and Lord of lords!
Amen.

52

Surprised to see them there?

Annas and Caiaphas

Then he led them out as far as Bethany, and, lifting up his hands, he blessed them. While he was blessing them, he withdrew from them and was carried up into heaven. And they worshipped him, and returned to Jerusalem with great joy; and they were continually in the temple blessing God.

Luke 24:50–53

Meditation

Annas Surprised to see them there?
Caiaphas You bet we were!
Annas They were the *last* people we expected to turn up,
given what had happened to Jesus!
Caiaphas And the extraordinary thing is, it wasn't a one-off:
Annas they were there in the Temple *continually* –
Caiaphas hour after hour,
Annas day after day –
Caiaphas unable, apparently, to get enough of the place.
Annas But if you think *that's* odd,
let me tell you something stranger still:
they were *glorying and praising God,*
Caiaphas smiles on their faces as wide as the Temple itself!
Annas Of course, we encourage that sort of thing usually,
but, since that leader of theirs had been nailed to a cross
just weeks earlier,
you'd have thought they'd have been in mourning,
wouldn't you?
Caiaphas Not a bit of it though:
they were as happy as the day is long.
Annas How do you explain that?
Caiaphas Were they simply thankful to have emerged unscathed,
to be spared the fate of their master?

Annas Possibly,
but there seemed more to it than that:
Caiaphas almost as though they felt that Jesus was still with them –
that he'd been vindicated and had won the day.
Annas We thought we'd seen the back of him, once and for all,
Caiaphas for they'd been desolate,
Annas despairing,
Caiaphas utterly crushed,
Annas any hopes and dreams they may have had,
sealed with him in a tomb.
Caiaphas But then someone made off with his body –
Annas don't ask us how –
Caiaphas and they seem now to revere him more than ever –
to worship him as God himself!
Annas I don't know what's changed them,
but it must be something truly remarkable,
out of this world.
Caiaphas We just can't work it out.
Annas Can *you*?

Prayer

Sovereign Saviour,
thank you that you brought faith down to earth,
literally,
revealing God in human form,
his greatness and glory in a way we can understand
and relate to one to one.
Help us to celebrate that truth,
but to remember also that you are exalted on high,
enthroned beside the Father.
Though, then, we can greet you as a friend,
teach us also to worship you as King of kings
and Lord of lords,
offering our love, faith and service in grateful praise
and humble worship.
Amen.

53

We thought we'd lost him

The Apostle James

When he had said this, as they were watching, he was lifted up, and a cloud took him out of their sight.

Acts 1:9

Meditation

We thought we'd lost him.
After everything we'd been through
we thought we'd lost him.
And it was dreadful.
It had been terrible enough the first time –
watching helplessly from the shadows as he was crucified,
as he was cut down from the cross,
as they laid him in that tomb.
We'd believed it was all over –
the end of a wonderful adventure –
and we were devastated,
inconsolable.
Only then he came back.
Astonishingly,
incredibly,
he came back!
And we were together once more,
almost like in the old days,
life suddenly magical again,
even more than it had been before.
Until he left us –
by our sides one minute,
gone the next!
We couldn't work it out at all,
just stood there,
gazing up at the clouds,
tears streaming down our faces.
He'd left us to face the world alone,

abandoned us when we needed him most.
Why?
How could he do it?
That's what we kept on asking.
But then a strange feeling came over us.
I can't explain it;
it was almost like a voice from heaven.
And when we looked at each other again
we somehow knew he *hadn't* gone,
not really.
Even though we wouldn't see him again,
wouldn't be able to walk and talk with him as we used to,
we knew he was there with us;
there in Jerusalem, Galilee, Judea and Samaria,
in all the world,
wherever we might choose to go.
And we knew he would be with us every moment,
even in death itself,
waiting to receive us and welcome us home.
We thought we'd lost him,
and for a moment it was dreadful.
But the fact is we had to lose him
before we could really find him.

Prayer

Lord Jesus Christ,
we greet you as King of kings and Lord of lords.
We acknowledge your greatness,
we recognise your authority,
we celebrate your exaltation,
we commit ourselves to your kingdom.
Living Lord,
open our eyes to the meaning of your ascension.
Broaden our vision,
enlarge our understanding,
widen our perspectives,
deepen our faith.
Equip us for all you would have us do,
so that may we live to your glory
and work for your kingdom.
Amen.

54

We stood there, speechless for a moment

The Apostle James

While he was going and they were gazing up towards heaven, suddenly two men in white robes stood by them. They said, 'Men of Galilee, why do you stand looking up toward heaven? This Jesus, who has been taken up from you into heaven, will come in the same way as you saw him go into heaven.'

Acts 1:10, 11

Meditation

We stood there, speechless for a moment,
struck dumb by the enormity of it all,
for he was gone,
plucked away from before our very eyes
and, quite simply, we were lost for words,
stunned into silence.
It wasn't the first time, you see;
we'd lost him once already –
watched in horror as he was nailed to a cross, sealed in a tomb,
and we'd been devastated,
convinced we could never bounce back from such a blow.
We wouldn't have, either,
not by ourselves,
but suddenly he was back,
there in the garden,
there on the roadside,
there in the upper room –
our Lord, alive, risen, victorious,
death unable to hold him!
I just can't tell you how wonderful that was,
how our hearts skipped and spirits soared
each time we saw him.
We felt certain nothing could ever again destroy our happiness,
for he had taken on the last enemy

and emerged triumphant!
Life, all at once, pulsated with promise,
no problem too great for us,
no challenge too daunting,
for, with Christ by our side, what had we to fear?
Yet suddenly, as we stood there that day gazing into heaven,
he was by our side no longer,
and for an awful moment
it seemed as though all our hopes had disappeared again,
vanishing with him like a bubble on the wind.
Only, of course, this time was different,
for we'd made time to listen,
paid heed to his warnings,
and we understood that, as he had departed,
so finally he would return.
You should see us now;
our faith, if anything, is stronger today than it's ever been!
We've spoken more boldly and witnessed more powerfully
than I thought possible –
preaching the word,
healing the sick,
renewing the weak,
uplifting the broken-hearted,
carrying the good news of Jesus far and wide.
And I'll tell you why:
because his going that day
has somehow brought him closer than he's ever been before,
filling our whole being –
body, mind and soul –
transforming our every thought and word and deed.
He's here,
he's there,
he's everywhere,
no person beyond his love,
no situation beyond his purpose,
for he has not simply risen,
he has ascended –
Jesus, the man who lived and died amongst us,
who shared our flesh and blood,
one with the Father,
Lord of lords and King of kings,

nothing in heaven or earth able to separate us
from the wonder of his love.
And sometimes when I think of all that means,
once more I'm struck dumb,
stunned into silence by the enormity of it all,
for it's wonderful, isn't it? –
almost too wonderful for words!

Prayer

Lord Jesus Christ,
you were brought low,
yet you have been lifted high.
You were the servant of all,
yet you are above all and beyond all.
You were despised and rejected,
yet your name is exalted above all names.
You were fully human,
yet you are divine.
You were taken into heaven,
yet you are here by our sides.
You are higher than our highest thoughts,
greater than our minds can ever grasp.
So, with all your people in every age,
we bow before you and confess you as our risen Saviour,
the King of kings and Lord of lords,
to the glory of God the Father.
Amen.

Pentecost

55

We felt abandoned

The Apostle John

'I will not leave you orphaned; I am coming to you. In a little while the world will no longer see me, but you will see me; because I live, you also will live.'

John 14:18, 19

Meditation

We felt abandoned,
bereft –
like orphans in a hostile and dangerous world.
To see Jesus arrested like that,
flogged, crucified and laid in a tomb –
it was like losing a parent, partner and friend all in one,
for we'd loved him beyond all others,
his presence giving meaning to life,
light to our path.
But then he returned,
just as he'd promised –
risen,
victorious,
yet the same old Jesus we'd known before.
He walked with us,
talked with us,
and for a moment it was as though nothing had happened.
But it *had*, of course,
for he'd defeated death,
vanquished evil,
his place no longer with *us* but with the Father,
enthroned on high.
He knew it,
we knew it,
and so it proved,
our Lord taken from us again . . .

but we're not abandoned,
not alone,
for once more,
just as he promised,
he's present among us,
his Spirit within,
to the end of time.

Prayer

Saviour Christ,
thank you for the promise of your return,
the knowledge that, in the fullness of time,
you will come again to establish your kingdom
and to welcome all your people, from every place and time,
into the joy of your kingdom.
But thank you also that you have come again already,
not just in the miracle of your resurrection
but in the equally miraculous gift of your Holy Spirit,
dwelling within,
making you known.
Thank you for, through that Spirit,
touching our hearts and transforming our lives –
enabling,
inspiring,
teaching,
guiding –
bringing faith to birth
and sustaining it across the years.
Open our hearts to the Spirit's work,
and make us wholly yours.
Amen.

56

It happened, just as he had promised

Peter

'If you love me, you will keep my commandments. And I will ask the Father, and he will give you another Advocate, to be with you for ever. This is the Spirit of truth, whom the world cannot receive, because it neither sees him nor knows him. You know him, because he abides with you, and he will be in you. But the Advocate, the Holy Spirit, whom the Father will send in my name, will teach you everything, and remind you of all that I have said to you.'

John 14:15–17, 26

Meditation

It happened, just as he had promised,
the Spirit coming upon us
to transform our lives.
One moment we were weak,
the next strong,
first timid,
then suddenly bold –
faith that we'd hidden away now shouted from the rooftops,
joyfully and proudly proclaimed.
We'd been changed,
outwardly and within,
God's living presence kindling faith and equipping for service,
inspiring faith, hope, love and joy.
And there's more,
much more –
gifts to build us up,
fruits to mark us out –
his power continuing to shape all we do
and all we are.
Jesus is gone,
yet he's *here* with us;
is far,

yet he's always near –
teaching,
guiding,
enabling,
inspiring,
just as he did before.
It happened as he promised,
the Spirit coming from on high,
and it's happening still,
all around.
Open you heart and receive in turn:
Christ in you
and you in him.

Prayer

Come among us, Lord, through your Spirit,
and touch our lives.
Give strength in our weakness,
and faith in our doubt,
turning our fear to trust,
our sorrow to joy
and our darkness to light.
Cleanse,
renew,
inspire,
equip,
so that we may live and work for you,
in your power
and for your glory.
Amen.

57

A mighty wind, some point to

The Apostle James

Jesus said to them again, 'Peace be with you. As the Father has sent me, so I send you.' When he had said this, he breathed on them and said to them, 'Receive the Holy Spirit.'

John 20:21, 22

Meditation

A mighty wind, some point to,
tongues of fire,
as though *that* was the moment the Spirit came,
dramatic and unmistakable.
They're half right of course,
for that Pentecost experience *was* special,
transforming not only our lives,
but also the world,
for ever.
Yet the turning point came earlier,
when, as we huddled behind locked doors,
lost and fearful,
Jesus appeared from nowhere and breathed new life –
resurrection life –
into our hearts.
No fuss,
no fireworks,
but suddenly we felt different –
energised and enthused,
yet also strangely tranquil,
at peace with ourselves and with God.
It was part of his special gift,
his presence within us,
teaching,
guiding,
enabling,

inspiring:
one moment, signs and wonders,
the next, quiet nurture;
one minute, sending us out,
the next, working within.
You can't tie it down,
nor should you try,
for the Spirit blows where it will,
poured out on us,
on you,
on all:
a gust of wind yet a gentle breeze,
a breath of fresh air,
God's kiss of life.

Prayer

Mighty God,
we praise you for the activity, experience and power of your Spirit,
making real your presence within our hearts.
We celebrate how, through that Spirit,
you give us guidance, instruction and insight;
how you challenge and inspire,
nurturing and nourishing our faith
and equipping us for service.
Above all, we rejoice that the Spirit works
not according to our own wishes –
directed by any merit, deserving or ingenuity on our part –
but by your will,
moving at your behest and fulfilling your purpose.
Fill, renew, shape and transform us,
to the glory of your name.
Amen.

58

'You will be my witnesses'

The Apostle John

'This,' he said, 'is what you have heard from me; for John baptised with water, but you will be baptised with the Holy Spirit not many days from now . . . You will receive power when the Holy Spirit comes upon you; and you will be my witnesses in Jerusalem, in all Judea and Samaria, and to the ends of the earth.'

Acts 1:4b, 5, 8

Meditation

'You will be my witnesses
in Jerusalem,
in all Judea and Samaria,
and to the ends of the earth.'
Quite a picture, isn't it,
a prospect to stir the heart and fire the imagination.
But I tell you what,
huddled there together in that upper room,
those words seemed a long way off,
a beautiful but rapidly fading memory.
We were terrified of going out, if the truth be told,
despite our prayers,
despite his promise,
scared stiff our enemies would come for us
as they'd come for him,
and send us off to some equally ghastly death.
We wished it were different, of course we did –
we longed for courage to get out there
and proclaim the good news,
to tell the world what Christ had done,
but, even if we had found that courage,
it wouldn't have counted for much,
for we had no idea what to say or how to say it.
We were twelve men with a mission –

and none of us had the first idea where to start,
let alone where it all might finish!
So we just sat there,
and waited,
and hoped,
longing to believe it might be true
but in our heart of hearts wondering if it ever could be –
for who were we,
ordinary folk like us,
to set the world on fire?
It was an unlikely prospect, to say the least.
Only, suddenly, out of the blue, it happened,
a sound like a mighty rushing wind filling the room,
tongues of fire leaping and dancing upon us,
and, all at once, an ecstasy beyond words,
a peace, joy and confidence that defied description.
No more fear or doubt,
no more hesitation –
our mouths were opened and we spoke boldly,
moving out among the multitude that had gathered,
the words flowing freely as we needed them,
and all who heard us were amazed,
bewildered to hear us speaking in their own tongue.
A one-minute wonder?
Don't you believe it!
It was the beginning of an astonishing adventure,
a lifetime of witness,
an incredible journey of discipleship
out into Jerusalem,
on to Judea and Samaria,
and beyond, to the ends of the earth.
As I say, quite a picture, isn't it?
One to stir even the coldest heart
and fire the poorest of imaginations.
At least I hope it does,
for the job's not over, not by a long way,
nor, praise God, is the promise.
The call is there, and the offer is there,
for you and anyone who believes –
the promise of power to be witnesses to the risen Christ.
Wait patiently,

trust in the promise of the Father,
and you, like us, will receive.

Prayer

Lord,
it's hard to share our faith with a few,
let alone many.
When we listen to your call
to be witnesses to the ends of the earth
we feel that the task is hopelessly beyond us,
our resources feebly inadequate to meet the challenge.
Yet that is to view things from *our* perspective
rather than yours,
for you do not leave us dependent on our strength
but rather equip us with the power of the Holy Spirit
who is able to work in ways far exceeding our expectations.
Move within us,
as you have moved in your people across the centuries,
and teach us to trust you for the help we need,
when we need it.
Amen.

59

Did it go to my head, becoming an apostle like that?

Matthias

So they proposed two, Joseph called Barsabbas, who was also known as Justus, and Matthias. Then they prayed and said, 'Lord, you know everyone's heart. Show us which one of these two you have chosen to take the place in this ministry and apostleship from which Judas turned aside to go to his own place.' And they cast lots for them, and the lot fell on Matthias; and he was added to the eleven apostles.

Acts 1:23–26

Meditation

Did it go to my head, becoming an apostle like that?
Well, yes, I think it possibly did,
for a time anyway.
It was a rare honour, after all,
the ultimate accolade,
so undoubtedly there was a certain swagger in my step
for those first few days;
I'd hardly have been human if there hadn't been.
But it didn't last long,
for I soon came to realise that, if *I* had my role,
others had theirs,
just as important,
just as necessary to the work of the kingdom.
It wasn't a question of us and them,
the select few lording it over the many –
we were part of a team,
each with our own gifts to contribute,
our own strengths and our own weaknesses,
each depending on the other, as Christ depended on us.
We did try putting labels on people for a time, it's true –
deacons, teachers, prophets, apostles –

but it didn't work,
for though the ministries were real enough,
the Spirit couldn't be tied down to them,
neatly pigeon-holed for our convenience.
He was working through all, irrespective of our boundaries,
now here,
now there,
each day new surprises forcing us to think again,
new evidence of his power compelling us to take stock
and to broaden our horizons.
We're *all* special, every one of us,
all called to share in his ministry,
continue his work –
a priesthood of believers,
company of saints,
the body of Christ.
I wasn't to be a star after all,
but it didn't matter –
how could it, so long as Christ was proclaimed
and his love made known?
What counted, then as now, is that *I* did my bit,
and that *you* do yours.

Prayer

Lord,
it's easy to overvalue our gifts
and equally easy to undervalue them;
to have too high or too low an opinion of ourselves.
Help us to recognise that you value all equally,
each having something to contribute *to* others
and something to receive *from* them.
Teach us, then, to appreciate our own worth
and to recognise that of those around us,
and so may we learn to use the various gifts you have given
wisely and with humility
in the service of your kingdom.
Amen.

60

We shouldn't have been surprised

Peter

When the day of Pentecost had come, they were all together in one place. And suddenly from heaven there came a sound like the rush of a violent wind, and it filled the entire house where they were sitting. Divided tongues, as of fire, appeared among them, and a tongue rested on each of them. All of them were filled with the Holy Spirit and began to speak in other languages, as the Spirit gave them ability.

Acts 2:1–4

Meditation

We shouldn't have been surprised,
not if we'd had any sense;
it was what we'd been told to expect,
what he'd promised us.
But we never imagined anything quite so extraordinary.
We were waiting, it's true,
gathered together as so often before,
but we'd been doing that for days
and our confidence had taken a hammering.
We were going through the motions, that's all,
telling each other he hadn't forgotten us;
talking of the future as though we still believed in it
yet wondering in our hearts if there was anything to look forward to.
I mean, what could we hope to achieve when all was said and done.
What reason to think that we, a motley bunch if ever there was one,
should fare better than our master?
We wanted to carry on his work, don't get me wrong:
we wanted to tell people what had happened,
help them find faith for themselves,
but how could we even hope to begin?
So we kept the doors locked
and sang our hymns
and said our prayers
and hid our doubts.

Until suddenly it happened!
I can't properly describe it even now,
but it changed our lives.
It was as though a mighty wind blew away the cobwebs,
a refreshing breeze revived our flagging faith,
a breath of air stirred our spirits.
As though a tiny spark rekindled our confidence,
a tongue of fire set our hearts aflame,
a raging inferno swept away our fears.
As though life had begun again,
the world become a different place,
and each of us been born anew.
I know that doesn't make sense,
but it's the best I can do.
You'll have to experience it for yourself to understand.
And you can, just as we did.
Believe me, we never would have thought it possible,
despite all Jesus said to us.
We were lost,
lonely,
frightened,
hopelessly aware of our weaknesses,
searching for any strengths.
We never thought we'd change a soul,
let alone the world,
but that's because we had no idea how God could change *us*!

Prayer

Gracious God,
thank you for extraordinary moments that change our lives,
giving us joy and fulfilment we never imagined possible.
Thank you especially for the great gift of your Holy Spirit –
an experience that transformed the lives of the apostles,
that has changed the lives of countless believers across the centuries,
and that has power to reshape our lives here and now.
Open our hearts, minds and souls to your living presence
so that we shall know your life-changing power for ourselves.
Amen.

61

I don't know who was the more surprised

Peter

Now there were devout Jews from every nation under heaven living in Jerusalem. And at this sound the crowd gathered and was bewildered, because each one heard them speaking in the native language of each. Amazed and astonished, they asked, 'Are not all these who are speaking Galileans? And how is it that we hear, each of us, in our own native language?' All were amazed and perplexed, saying to one another, 'What does this mean?' But others sneered and said, 'They are filled with new wine.'

Acts 2:5–8, 12, 13

Meditation

I don't know who was the more surprised,
us, or them?
They were bewildered, certainly,
unable to make head or tail of what was going on,
amazed to hear us speaking to them in their own language
and wondering what on earth it all could mean.
But, if anything, *our* astonishment was the greater,
each of us scarcely able to believe what was happening.
Yes, I know we'd been told to expect it,
the promise having been given by Christ himself,
but as to what it meant,
what it actually involved,
we'd no idea until that incredible moment when the Spirit came.
No warning,
no tell-tale signs,
just bang! –
and our lives were changed for ever.
Truthfully, I never thought I had it in me,
to get out there and speak fearlessly for Christ –
and as for sharing in his ministry,
continuing where he had left off,
the very idea seemed ridiculous.

Only that's what happened –
gifts beyond our wildest imagining,
power beyond our most fantastic dreams,
a joy that burned unquenchably within us
and a sense of purpose that nothing could contain.
We were no longer on our own, gazing wistfully to the heavens –
Christ was with us,
and in a way more wonderful than he'd ever been before;
not just by our side,
but in our hearts,
filling our whole being with his presence.
It was more than we'd ever expected,
more than any of us had dared hope for,
and we had to pinch ourselves to be sure it was true.
But it was,
and I tell you what,
impossible though it seems,
I shouldn't wonder if God has more yet in store,
new experiences of his love,
new expressions of his purpose,
not just for us but for everyone,
his Spirit poured out on all, just as the prophet said –
nothing will surprise us now!

Prayer

Gracious God,
we are reminded today of the power of your Spirit,
through which, across the years,
you have fired ordinary people like us
to live and work for you
in joyful faith and fearless service.
Help us to know today, through that same Spirit,
that you are able to take any person,
any place,
any moment,
any situation,
and achieve within each of them things far more wonderful
than we can ever begin to imagine.
Amen.

62

It wasn't much of a gift

Barnabas

There was a Levite, a native of Cyprus, Joseph, to whom the apostles gave the name Barnabas (which means 'son of encouragement'). He sold a field that belonged to him, then brought the money, and laid it at the apostles' feet.

Acts 4:36, 37

Meditation

It wasn't much of a gift;
at least I didn't think so.
In fact, I didn't feel I had a gift at all,
not like the rest of them with all their stunning signs and wonders.
I envied them sometimes,
so often in the limelight,
stealing all the headlines –
prophets,
teachers,
workers of miracles,
speakers of tongues.
They were the ones who drew the crowds,
the ones who people noticed,
and all I did was plod quietly along,
living the faith in my own simple way,
speaking and doing and caring and sharing
as I believed Christ would have me do.
And then they gave me this name;
Barnabas, meaning 'son of encouragement'.
It was all so unexpected,
a complete surprise,
for what had I done to deserve any such honour.
But then they told me,
one by one,
that of all the gifts they valued,

mine was chief among them.
A generous gesture,
word of praise,
expression of trust,
act of love –
nothing to cause gasps or make heads turn –
these, they told me
had stirred their hearts and cheered their spirits
as signs and wonders could never do.
It doesn't seem much, does it –
encouraging people?
Not a gift you'll find in any of the textbooks,
nor one people will ever fight over.
Yet don't let that fool you as it did me.
If you're wondering, as I did, why you've been left out,
let me offer you some simple words of encouragement:
God's Spirit is often at work when we're least aware of it,
active through simple everyday gifts as much as showy ones.
Noticed or otherwise, such gifts are just as real,
just as necessary,
and equally special.

Prayer

Loving God,
when we read the pages of Scripture,
when we hear dramatic stories of testimony,
when we meet sparkling Christians,
it's hard sometimes not to feel a little daunted.
We don't have stunning gifts ourselves,
don't make the headlines,
and don't have exciting stories to tell.
Yet you remind us through people like Barnabas
that those behind the scenes with the unsung gifts
can make just as great a contribution to your kingdom as any other.
For that truth, thank you.
Amen.

63

I have to tell you!

Philip

Now those who were scattered went from place to place, proclaiming the word. Philip went down to the city of Samaria and proclaimed the Messiah to them. The crowds with one accord listened eagerly to what was said by Philip, hearing and seeing the signs that he did, for unclean spirits, crying with loud shrieks, came out of many who were possessed; and many others who were paralysed or lame were cured. So there was great joy in that city.

Acts 8:4–8

Meditation

I have to tell you!
Forgive me if I'm intruding,
barging in where I'm not wanted,
but I have to tell you what Christ has done for me.
I'm not bragging, God forbid!
There's been no merit on my part,
nothing about me that's special or deserving of praise.
I'm just an ordinary, everyday person,
no different from anyone else,
but I've suddenly discovered what really matters in life,
what really counts.
I thought I knew already;
well, we all do, don't we?
A good job,
loving partner,
nice home,
children –
you know the sort of thing.
And don't think I'm knocking those,
for they can all be precious,
all offer their own fulfilment.
But when I heard about Jesus,

met him for myself,
suddenly I discovered there is something else,
something more important than any of those,
able to give a whole new perspective on them all
and to answer my deepest needs.
I was set free from myself,
my guilt,
my sin,
my shame;
not suddenly becoming perfect
but finding forgiveness,
a new beginning,
a multitude of new beginnings.
I was set free from the endless quest for pleasure,
from the gods of greed, lust, pride and envy,
learning there is more to life than the thirst for gain
or pursuit of success.
I was set free from fear, worry, despair and sorrow,
even in my darkest days certain that joy will surely come.
And, above all, I've been freed from death,
knowing that, though this life will end, I shall rise again!
So now do you see why I have to tell,
have to let you know?
I've found so much;
such hope,
such peace,
such happiness;
and I can't just sit on that as though it's mine and mine alone.
I have to pass it on,
share it out,
let you find it too;
so forgive me if I'm intruding,
but if you've got a moment,
please, please,
let me tell you!

Prayer

Lord Jesus Christ,
you have called each of us to bear witness to what you have done,
and every day you give us countless opportunities to do just that.
You don't expect us to be gifted evangelists,
but you do ask us to speak naturally of you
when the chance presents itself.
Yet, more often than we care to remember,
when such opportunities have come we have wasted them,
uncertain what to say,
worried about making fools of ourselves,
afraid of rejection.
Forgive us all the occasions we have failed you,
and next time help us to speak freely,
knowing you will give us the words to say when we need them.
Amen.

64

It was all so unnecessary

The Apostle Paul

Now, concerning spiritual gifts, brothers and sisters, I do not want you to be uninformed . . . There are varieties of gifts, but the same Spirit; and there are varieties of services, but the same Lord; and there are varieties of activities, but it is the same God who activates all of them in everyone . . . For just as the body is one and has many members, and all the members of the body, though many, are one body, so it is with Christ . . . Now you are the body of Christ and individually members of it. And God has appointed in the church first apostles, second prophets, third teachers; then deeds of power, then gifts of healing, forms of assistance, forms of leadership, various kinds of tongues. Are all apostles? Are all prophets? Are all teachers? Do all work miracles? Do all possess gifts of healing? Do all speak in tongues? Do all interpret? But strive for the greater gifts. And I will show you a still more excellent way.

1 Corinthians 12:1, 4–6, 12, 27–31

Meditation

It was all so unnecessary,
such a senseless stupid waste –
grown men and women who should have known better,
arguing amongst each other,
almost coming to blows,
and all over so-called gifts of the Spirit.
Well, some gifts they turned out to be!
I could hardly believe it –
so much anger and bitterness,
just because people experienced God differently.
Why couldn't they see the other's point of view:
recognise that some need to express themselves one way,
others another;
some have this gift,
others one completely different?
Why turn it into a competition,
a test of spiritual blessing?

It wouldn't have been so bad had it been over something important –
our failure to love,
inability to forgive,
weakness in discipleship.
But this –
it was all finally so trivial,
the whole business peripheral
to what should really have concerned us.
Oh, I don't deny such gifts have their place –
a time and a season for everything –
but when they divide rather than bring together,
upset rather than uplift,
surely something has to be wrong somewhere?
Yet they just wouldn't have it,
each vying to outdo the other,
jostling to claim the most spectacular gift,
the profoundest blessing.
Couldn't they see the damage they were doing,
the message they broadcast to the world?
Didn't they realise that every dispute, every division,
broke again the body of Christ,
inflicting yet more suffering upon him?
Apparently not.
They were tearing themselves apart,
slowly but surely destroying the unity
that he had suffered such agony to bring them,
and all in the name of his Spirit.
Don't think I blame one above the other;
I don't.
They were all to blame,
each as intolerant as the next,
denying through their deeds what they claimed with their lips.
It's up to them now;
I've done my best,
tried to get the message home.
They can go on feuding if they want to,
no place for anyone but themselves,
but when the day comes when they're finally called to account,
and they find, then,
that there's no place for anyone *like* themselves,
don't say I didn't warn them!

Prayer

Lord,
we each have *some* gifts,
but none of us has them *all*.
We each have something to contribute to others,
and equally something to receive from them,
and our lives are impoverished if we attempt to go it alone.
You call us all to be part of your body
with a unique role to play within that,
but by the same token we belong to an interdependent whole
in which every member is of vital importance.
Teach us, then, not only to exercise our own gifts wisely
but at the same time to appreciate those of others,
and so may we grow together,
building one another up in love,
to the glory of your name.
Amen.

65

He taught me the meaning of love

The Apostle Paul

If I speak in the tongues of mortals and of angels, but do not have love, I am a noisy gong or a clanging cymbal. And if I have prophetic powers, and understand all mysteries and all knowledge, and if I have all faith, so as to remove mountains, but do not have love, I am nothing. If I give away all my possessions, and if I hand over my body so that I may boast, but do not have love, I gain nothing. Love is patient; love is kind; love is not envious or boastful or arrogant or rude. It does not insist on its own way; it is not irritable or resentful; it does not rejoice in wrongdoing, but rejoices in the truth. It bears all things, believes all things, hopes all things, endures all things. And now faith, hope, and love abide, these three; and the greatest of these is love.

1 Corinthians 13:1–7, 13

Meditation

He taught me the meaning of love,
what it really means to say, 'I love you'.
Slowly,
gently,
he taught me.
Not through words,
nor through gestures,
but through showing me love in action.
I thought I'd understood,
that I loved as much as the next man, maybe more.
Not perhaps as a husband loves his wife, or a father his children –
there's not been time for that, sadly –
but deeper,
beyond such natural ties.
And I did love in my own way, of course I did –
my single aim being to help them,
serve them,
reach them.
And yet, despite all that, I sometimes wondered if I'd ever loved at all,

for deep down, in my heart of hearts, I knew it was all about me –
my preaching, *my* striving, *my* loving;
my efforts, *my* successes, *my* ambitions –
all finally for my own satisfaction
and even, I fear, my own glory as much as his.
It's human, I realise that, or so at least we tell ourselves,
but is that true?
Or does it have to be?
For when I look at Jesus,
all he did for me,
I see a different truth,
a different kind of love;
patient, kind, humble;
not serving self or seeking gain,
but putting others first.
A love that knows me as I am,
understands my faults,
yet still believes in me.
A love that, though I turn away, accepts me,
even dies for me!
That's what it means, this thing called love:
seeing the worst,
believing the best,
asking nothing,
and giving all.
I thought I'd understood, all those years ago,
but I hadn't, hardly at all.
I'm still learning even now,
still struggling to let go of self.
I can't do it alone,
I've come to realise that at last;
I need his help, his love flowing through me,
and I'll carry on praying for that,
striving for that,
until my dying day,
for I understand now that without love all else is nothing.

Prayer

Lord Jesus Christ,
you summed up the Law in one simple word: 'love'.
Forgive us that we make the gospel so complicated.
And forgive us that, though we talk so often about love,
we all too rarely practise it.
Help us to look to you who showed us love in action –
a love that bears all things,
believes all things,
hopes all things,
endures all things.
And help us truly to realise
that unless we have such love in our hearts
then all our words, all our faith, and all our religion
count for nothing.
Amen.

Trinity Sunday

66

I didn't know if I was coming or going

Nicodemus

Jesus answered, 'Very truly, I tell you, no one can enter the kingdom of God without being born of water and Spirit. What is born of the flesh is flesh, and what is born of the Spirit is spirit. Do not be astonished that I said to you, "You must be born from above." The wind blows where it chooses, and you hear the sound of it, but you do not know where it comes from or where it goes. So it is with everyone who is born of the Spirit.' Nicodemus said to him, 'How can these things be?'

John 3:5–9

Meditation

I didn't know if I was coming or going.
One moment he was talking about himself,
the next, of God,
and the next, of the Spirit,
almost as though they were same thing.
I'd seen already that God was working through him,
even if my fellow Pharisees struggled with the idea –
how else could you explain what he was doing?
But as we talked together, he seemed to imply more than that:
that he spoke for the Father himself,
and somehow, in his own person, brought the Spirit among us.
I was baffled, mystified,
yet he didn't seem surprised –
if anything, the opposite.
Oh, he teased me a little,
pointing out that, as a teacher of Israel,
I, of all people, should have known such things,
but, if I understand him correctly,
he didn't so much expect me to unravel the mystery
as to accept that I can't;
to realise that it *is* a mystery, and always will be.
God as three persons –

could he seriously be suggesting that?
It's preposterous, surely,
even blasphemy,
yet somehow I've not been able to dismiss it from my mind,
for in a strange way it seems to make sense.
He *did* show me God, as no other has done,
and the Spirit moved not only through *him*,
but also through those followers of his,
almost as though he'd passed it on
and was still with them after he'd died.
It's hard to believe,
impossible to believe:
that God is three in one yet one in three.
Yet do you know what?
I really think it's true!

Prayer

Almighty God,
teach us to live with the mystery of who you are,
to recognise that though we can never fully articulate,
let alone understand,
the wonder of your being,
we can experience it nonetheless,
responding to you each day as Father, Son and Holy Spirit.
However much it defies logic
and stretches imagination to the limit,
may we know and honour you as God above us,
God beside us,
God within us,
three in one yet one in three.
Help us to worship you in all your splendour,
glimpsing in your varied faces the Lord of all,
your glory filling the universe
yet touching our lives,
your purpose transcending space and time
yet enfolding us in eternity.
Almighty God,
different yet ever the same,
we praise you.
Amen.

67

'What's in a name?' people ask

Matthew

'Go therefore and make disciples of all nations, baptising them in the name of the Father and of the Son and of the Holy Spirit.'

Matthew 28:19

Meditation

'What's in a name?' people ask,
and, of course, it depends –
some chosen at random,
some full of meaning;
some just a label,
others a clue to the person beneath.
For *us*, names mattered,
the following in particular:
Father,
Son
and Holy Spirit –
definitely more than labels,
speaking of one yet three.
God the Father,
our Father:
the one who gave us life,
who brought to birth everything that is
and has been
and shall be –
who creates,
sustains,
provides
and nurtures,
helping his children to grow.
God the Son,
flesh and blood,
the divine with a human face:

sharing our laughter,
our tears,
our life,
our death;
the one who stood in our place
that we might rise to his.
God the Holy Spirit,
free as the wind,
moving where it will,
moving within;
the one who teaches,
inspires,
guides,
transforms –
imparting gifts,
producing fruits.
Three names,
one God;
three persons,
one truth;
each complete,
yet reduced without the other;
each separate,
yet all joined.
What's in a name?
More than you may think.
Introduce yourself and see.

Prayer

God the Father,
help us to honour you as such:
to live as your children,
trusting in your care, guidance and provision.
God the Son,
help us to honour you as such:
to live each day as your brothers and sisters,
trusting in your love, compassion and forgiveness.
God the Holy Spirit,
help us to honour you as such:
to live each day as your people,

trusting in your presence, peace and power.
Almighty and mysterious God,
one in three and three in one,
watch over us,
redeem us,
fill us
and make us wholly yours.
Amen.

68

I didn't know what he was on about at the time

The Apostle John

'When the Advocate comes, whom I will send to you from the Father, the Spirit of truth who comes from the Father, he will testify on my behalf. You also are to testify because you have been with me from the beginning.'

John 15:26, 27

Meditation

I didn't know what he was on about at the time,
not the faintest idea,
despite the way I nodded
and attempted to smile in the right places.
The Advocate?
The Son who comes from the Father?
What did it all mean?
We believed he was sent by God, yes –
called to reveal his will,
build his kingdom –
but was he saying more,
pointing to a closer relationship?
It seemed so,
yet, try as we might, we just couldn't get our heads round it.
'The Lord our God is one' –
isn't that what we'd always been told?
Indeed, he said it himself,
made no bones about it,
so how could he also tell us, 'He who has seen me
has seen the Father'?
We were baffled, there's no other word for it,
and when he went on to talk about the Spirit of truth,
the one his Father would send in his name,
quite simply, by then, we were reeling,

unable to make head or tail of what he was getting at.
'Do we understand now, though?' you ask.
Well, no, we don't actually.
Funnily enough, if we try to explain it
we still struggle as much as ever;
the more we try, the worse the knots we tie ourselves in.
Yet, strange though it may sound, it makes sense despite that –
for day after day, year after year, we've tasted the truth,
the reality of Father, Son and Holy Spirit.
We look up,
to the stars and the sky,
the wonder of the heavens,
and God is there, enthroned in splendour,
sovereign over all.
We look around,
at the world he's given –
its awesome beauty,
endless interest,
bountiful provision –
and he is there,
stretching out his hand in love,
inviting us to share in its wonder.
We look nearby, at family and friends,
beyond, to the nameless faces of the multitude,
and he is there,
giving and receiving,
waiting to feed and be fed.
We look within,
at our aching souls,
our pleading hearts,
and he is there,
breathing new life,
new purpose within us.
One God, yes,
but a God we meet in different guises,
different ways,
three in one and one in three.
It sounds odd, I know,
and take it from me, you'll never explain it,
no matter how you try,
yet don't worry, for what finally matters is this:
though words may fail you, the experience never will!

Prayer

Almighty God,
there are no words able to sum up your nature,
to say everything about you that needs to be said.
We do our best to express our faith,
but inevitably we fall short,
for you are greater than our minds can fathom,
ultimately defying human understanding.
Yet we experience your love day after day in a multitude of ways:
in the wonder of the heavens and beauty of the earth;
in the life, death and resurrection of Christ,
in the power of your Spirit working deep within,
each revealing different aspects of who and what you are.
Our minds reel at the mystery of it all,
yet our hearts rejoice in your presence.
Almighty God,
Father, Son and Holy Spirit,
receive our praise.
Amen!

69

He's done the impossible

The Apostle John

'I still have many things to say to you, but you cannot bear them now. When the Spirit of truth comes, he will guide you into all the truth; for he will not speak on his own, but will speak whatever he hears, and he will declare to you the things that are to come. He will glorify me, because he will take what is mine and declare it to you. All that the Father has is mine. For this reason I said that he will take what is mine and declare it to you.'

John 16:12–15

Meditation

He's done the impossible,
putting us right with God –
not through any deserving on our part,
but simply and solely through his grace,
his costly redeeming love.
The debt is cancelled,
barrier broken,
chasm between us bridged –
we are at one with the Father,
reconciled in Christ.
But if *that* seems amazing,
there's more still,
for our friend Jesus –
who walked our earth
and died our death –
is not just *at one* with God,
he *is* one.
It doesn't make sense, does it?
But it's true nonetheless,
for he's shown us the Father,
just as he said he would –
God's love and purpose revealed in the Word made flesh.
And if that's not enough,

Christ is here now,
working within us through his Spirit,
day after day energising,
teaching,
guiding,
empowering –
seeking to make us new.
Father, Son and Holy Spirit:
they don't just *point* to each other,
they *are* each other . . .
and yet they're not,
for each also is distinct,
the three, one,
yet the one, three.
Yes, I know what you're thinking:
'that really *is* impossible!'
And I know just how you feel.
But I know something else as well,
proven by experience across the years.
Impossible or not,
it's also true!

Prayer

Lord Jesus Christ,
Son of God,
thank you for helping us to know the Father,
to glimpse his face,
hear his voice,
see his glory.
Lord Jesus Christ,
the Word made flesh,
thank you for making God real,
present among us,
sharing our humanity,
our life and death,
and opening the way to your kingdom.
Lord Jesus Christ,
giver of life,
thank you for your Holy Spirit,
constantly at work,

in our lives,
in your Church,
in the world.
Living Lord,
we offer our thanks,
we give you our praise,
we pledge you our service.
Amen.

70

He was just a man, that's what I thought

Thomas

A week later his disciples were again in the house, and Thomas was with them. Although the doors were shut, Jesus came and stood among them and said, 'Peace be with you.' Then he said to Thomas, 'Put your finger here and see my hands. Reach out your hand and put it in my side. Do not doubt but believe.' Thomas answered him, 'My Lord and my God!' Jesus said to him, 'Have you believed because you have seen me? Blessed are those who have not seen and yet have come to believe.'

John 20:26–29

Meditation

He was just a man, that's what I thought.
A wonderful person,
fantastic teacher,
the most caring sort of bloke you could ever hope to meet,
but just a man.
And nothing wrong with that, of course;
it's not every day you meet someone as special.
In fact, thank God he *was* a man,
as much flesh and blood as we are.
He knew what it was to be human,
to share our hopes and fears,
joys and sorrows,
life and death.
He laughed as we do,
wept as we do,
suffered as we do.
I know, for I was with him for three years of his life.
But I'd thought that his life was over.
When they laid him in that tomb and rolled the stone across,
I'd really thought that was it.
Until something happened –
something astonishing, marvellous, incredible:

he appeared to me,
just as he'd appeared to the rest of the disciples,
large as life,
and I knew then that he wasn't just a man;
he was God!
I understood at last what he'd been on about before,
those words that had never made sense earlier:
'Whoever has seen me has seen the Father,
no one has ever seen God, but I have made him known to you.'
'Of course!' I said. 'Of course!'
and I fell down and worshipped him.
Do you know, God was more real to me then
than I'd ever dreamt he could be.
So when he disappeared again shortly afterwards,
you can imagine we were gutted.
It felt as though our world had fallen apart,
as though we'd been cut off from God.
But not for long,
for somehow it swiftly dawned on us
that he was with us after all,
nearer than he'd ever been before.
It didn't matter that we couldn't see him,
couldn't touch him.
We felt his presence deep inside,
guiding,
renewing,
working through us.
And again I remembered his words:
'The Holy Spirit, whom the Father will send in my name,
will teach you all things.
God is spirit, and those who worship him
must worship in spirit and in truth.'
He was a man, he really was,
as human as you and me.
But he was God,
showing us the Father.
And he's also Spirit –
God with us now, deep in our hearts.
You don't need my word for that,
you don't need anyone's,
for you can experience it for yourselves:
incredible, but true.

Prayer

Mighty God,
beyond all space and time,
greater than our minds can fully grasp,
ruler over all that is and has been and shall be,
we worship you.
We worship you as the God made known to us in Christ,
a God all good and wholly other,
and yet a God who loves us as a father loves his children,
a God who has shared our humanity.
We worship you as the God we experience within us,
the God who fires our imagination and sets our hearts aflame
through the Spirit of Christ.
Mighty God,
help us to catch a sense of your greatness,
opening our hearts and minds to your presence
made known through Father, Son and Holy Spirit.
Amen.

Index of Key Themes

apostles
  adding of Matthias to their number 157–8
  appearance of risen Christ to 50–76, 91–3, 187–8
ascension, of Christ 132–45

body of Christ, unity of 168–70
bread and wine, meeting Christ in 43, 45–8

changed lives 57–9, 139–40, 143–5, 150–51
  see also Holy Spirit: gift of

despair, transformed to hope 37–59, 79–81, 141–5, 148–9
  see also empty tomb
disbelief, at resurrection 19–21, 24–33, 60–71, 98–9, 119–21
  see also doubt, and faith
divinity, of Jesus *see* ascension, of Christ
division, over spiritual gifts 168–70
doubt, and faith 32–6, 52–71, 98–9
  see also disbelief, at resurrection

Emmaus road, meeting Jesus on 42–9
empty tomb, the 12–36
  see also resurrection, of Christ; tomb: attempts to guard
encouragement, gift of 163–4
eternal life, promise of 102–3, 117–29

fishers of men, call to be 72–3
  see also mission, call to
forgiveness, and new life 24–6, 91–3
fruitfulness, in discipleship 106–7

garden, Christ's appearance to Mary in 37–41
gentle touch, of the Spirit 152–3
gifts
  of ourselves and others 157–8
  in relation to body of Christ 168–70
  unsung 163–4
  see also Holy Spirit

glorification, of Christ 100–101, 113–14, 132–45
God, threefold nature of 176–89
guards, placed at tomb of Christ 82–91

heaven
glimpsed on earth 102–3, 117–18
nature of 122–4
vision of 125–9
Holy Spirit
dwelling within us 104–5
fruits of 106–7
gift of 148–56, 159–64
guiding of into truth 110–12
see also God, threefold nature of
horizons, broadening 100–101
see also ascension, of Christ; God, threefold nature of

journey of discipleship, Christ meeting us on 42–9
joy, gift of 115–16

knowledge of God, growth in 110–12
see also God, threefold nature of

love
as fulfilment of the Law 108–9
as greatest of gifts 171–3

mission, call to 72–3, 94–5, 119–21, 132–4, 154–6, 165–7
mystery, of faith *see* God, threefold nature of

new beginnings 69–71, 79–81, 91–3
see also changed lives; resurrection, of Christ

Pentecost, day of 152, 159–62
prophecy, resurrection as fulfilment of 74–8

questions of faith *see* God, threefold nature of

resurrection life, nature of 122–4
resurrection, of Christ 12–81, 91–3, 187–8

attempts to discredit 82–91
Paul's proclamation of 119–24

sacrificial love, of Christ 113–14
Scripture, resurrection foretold in 74–8
self-denial, of Christ 113–14
shepherd, Christ as 94–7
sorrow, transformed to joy 37–59, 79–81, 141–5, 148–9
see also empty tomb
Spirit *see* Holy Spirit

threefold nature of God 176–89
tomb
attempts to guard 82–91
empty 12–36
see also resurrection, of Christ

unity, Christian 168–70
unsung gifts 163–4

worth, of ourselves and others 157–8

Index of Principal Characters

Andrew 54–5, 74–5, 117–18
Annas 82–3
and Caiaphas 139–40
apostles, the 115–16

Barnabas 163–4
Bartholomew 57–8

Caiaphas 85–6
and Annas 139–40
Cleopas 42–3, 45–6, 48–9

Dionysius the Areopagite 119–20

guard, one of at the tomb 88–9

James, the Apostle 50–51, 69–70, 113–14, 141–2, 143–5, 152–3
and John and Peter 30–31, 110–11
Joanna, companion of the disciples 77–8
John, the Apostle 34–5, 148–9, 154–6, 181–2, 184–5
and James and Peter 30–31, 110–11
John, the Evangelist 125–6, 128–9

Mary Magdalene 22–3, 24–5, 37–8, 40–41, 79–80
Mary, the other 14–15
Matthew 67–8, 132–3, 178–9
Matthias 157–8

Nathanael 72–3
Nicodemus 176–7

Paul, the Apostle 122–3, 168–9, 171–2
Peter 27–8, 32–3, 52–3, 91–2, 137–8, 150–51, 159–60, 161–2
and James and John 30–31, 110–11
Philip 102–3, 104–5, 135–6, 165–6
and Thomas 108–9

Sadducee, listening to Jesus 98–9
Salome 12–13, 16–17, 19–20
shepherd, a 94–5, 96–7

Thomas 60–61, 63–4, 65–6, 100–101, 187–8
  and Philip 108–9
tomb, one of the guards at 88–9

vineyard owner, a 106–7

Index of Bible Passages

Matthew

28:1–3 14
28:9, 10 79
28:11 82, 85
28:12–15 88
28:16–20 132
28:19 178

Mark

16:1–4 12
16:4 16
16:8 19
16:9, 10 24
16:9–11 27
16:14 52

Luke

24:10, 11 30
24:12 32
24:13–18 42
24:30, 31 45
24:32–35 48
24:36–39 69
24:41–43 57
24:44 74
24:45–48 77
24:50, 51 135
24:50–53 139
24:52, 53 137

John

3:5–9 176
10:1–3 94
10:11–15 96
10:24–28 98
13:31–33 100
14:2–8 102
14:15–17, 26 150

14:18, 19 148
14:23, 25, 26 104
15:1, 2 106
15:9–12 108
15:26, 27 181
16:12–14 110
16:12–15 184
17:1, 6, 11 113
17:7, 8, 13 115
17:24, 26 117
20:1, 2 22
20:3–8 34
20:11a 37
20:11b–14 40
20:19, 20 50, 54
20:21, 22 152
20:24, 25 60, 65
20:26–28 63
20:26–29 187
20:28, 29 67
21:9–13 72
21:15–17 91

Acts
1:4b, 5, 8 154
1:9 141
1:10, 11 143
1:23–26 157
2:1–4 159
2:5–8, 12, 13 161
4:36, 37 163
8:4–8 165
17:22a, 30, 34 119

1 Corinthians
12:1, 4–6, 12, 27–31 168
13:1–7, 13 171
15:35, 36; 42–44a 122

Revelation
21:1–4 125
22:3–5 128